The Daily Prayer Journal For Women To Write In

A 365-Day Christian Devotional With Scripture Memory Verses Of The Day

Jessica Strauss

January

Faith Scriptures

JANUARY 1

Therefore I tell you, whatever you ask for in prayer, believe that you have received it, and it will be yours.
<u>Mark 11:24</u>

How Does This Scripture Speak To You?

_____

_____

_____

_____

_____

In What Ways Can You Apply This To Your Life?

_____

_____

_____

_____

_____

Who Could You Pray For Right Now Based On This Scripture?

_____

_____

_____

_____

JANUARY 2

I pray that out of his glorious riches he may strengthen you with power through his Spirit in your inner being, so that Christ may dwell in your hearts through faith. And I pray that you, being rooted and established in love. Ephesians 3:16-17

How Does This Scripture Speak To You?

_____
_____
_____
_____
_____

In What Ways Can You Apply This To Your Life?

_____
_____
_____
_____
_____

Who Could You Pray For Right Now Based On This Scripture?

_____
_____
_____
_____

JANUARY 3

Now faith is confidence in what we hope for and assurance about what we do not see.
Hebrews 11:1

How Does This Scripture Speak To You?

_____

_____

_____

_____

_____

In What Ways Can You Apply This To Your Life?

_____

_____

_____

_____

_____

Who Could You Pray For Right Now Based On This Scripture?

_____

_____

_____

_____

JANUARY 4

For we live by faith, not by sight.
2 Corinthians 5:7

How Does This Scripture Speak To You?

_____
_____
_____
_____
_____

In What Ways Can You Apply This To Your Life?

_____
_____
_____
_____
_____

Who Could You Pray For Right Now Based On This Scripture?

_____
_____
_____
_____

JANUARY 5

May the God of hope fill you with all joy and peace
as you trust in him, so that you may overflow with
hope by the power of the Holy Spirit.
Romans 15:13

How Does This Scripture Speak To You?

_____

_____

_____

_____

_____

In What Ways Can You Apply This To Your Life?

_____

_____

_____

_____

_____

Who Could You Pray For Right Now Based On This Scripture?

_____

_____

_____

_____

JANUARY 6

But when you ask, you must believe and not doubt,
because the one who doubts is like a wave of the sea,
blown and tossed by the wind.
James 1:6

How Does This Scripture Speak To You?

_____

_____

_____

_____

_____

In What Ways Can You Apply This To Your Life?

_____

_____

_____

_____

_____

Who Could You Pray For Right Now Based On This Scripture?

_____

_____

_____

_____

JANUARY 7

And without faith it is impossible to please God, because anyone who comes to him must believe that he exists and that he rewards those who earnestly seek him. Hebrews 11:6

How Does This Scripture Speak To You?

_____

_____

_____

_____

In What Ways Can You Apply This To Your Life?

_____

_____

_____

_____

Who Could You Pray For Right Now Based On This Scripture?

_____

_____

_____

JANUARY 8

Then Jesus said, "Did I not tell you that if you believe,
you will see the glory of God?"
John 11:40

How Does This Scripture Speak To You?

_____

_____

_____

_____

_____

In What Ways Can You Apply This To Your Life?

_____

_____

_____

_____

_____

Who Could You Pray For Right Now Based On This Scripture?

_____

_____

_____

_____

JANUARY 9

Though you have not seen him, you love him; and even though you do not see him now, you believe in him and are filled with an inexpressible and glorious joy, for you are receiving the end result of your faith, the salvation of your souls. 1 Peter 1:8-9

How Does This Scripture Speak To You?

_____

_____

_____

_____

_____

In What Ways Can You Apply This To Your Life?

_____

_____

_____

_____

_____

Who Could You Pray For Right Now Based On This Scripture?

_____

_____

_____

_____

JANUARY 10

Because you know that the testing of your faith
produces perseverance.
<u>James 1:3</u>

How Does This Scripture Speak To You?

_____
_____
_____
_____
_____

In What Ways Can You Apply This To Your Life?

_____
_____
_____
_____
_____

Who Could You Pray For Right Now Based On This Scripture?

_____
_____
_____
_____

JANUARY 11

"Everything is possible for one who believes."
Mark 9:23

How Does This Scripture Speak To You?

_____

_____

_____

_____

_____

In What Ways Can You Apply This To Your Life?

_____

_____

_____

_____

_____

Who Could You Pray For Right Now Based On This Scripture?

_____

_____

_____

_____

JANUARY 12

Jesus said to her, "I am the resurrection and the life. The one who believes in me will live, even though they die; and whoever lives by believing in me will never die. Do you believe this?" John 11:25-26

How Does This Scripture Speak To You?

_____
_____
_____
_____
_____

In What Ways Can You Apply This To Your Life?

_____
_____
_____
_____
_____

Who Could You Pray For Right Now Based On This Scripture?

_____
_____
_____
_____

JANUARY 13

Accept the one whose faith is weak, without quarreling over disputable matters.
Romans 14:1

How Does This Scripture Speak To You?

_____
_____
_____
_____
_____

In What Ways Can You Apply This To Your Life?

_____
_____
_____
_____
_____

Who Could You Pray For Right Now Based On This Scripture?

_____
_____
_____
_____

JANUARY 14

For everyone born of God overcomes the world. This is the victory that has overcome the world, even our faith. 1 John 5:4

How Does This Scripture Speak To You?

_____
_____
_____
_____
_____

In What Ways Can You Apply This To Your Life?

_____
_____
_____
_____
_____

Who Could You Pray For Right Now Based On This Scripture?

_____
_____
_____
_____

JANUARY 15

But you, man of God, flee from all this, and pursue righteousness, godliness, faith, love, endurance and gentleness. 1 Timothy 6:11

How Does This Scripture Speak To You?

_____
_____
_____
_____
_____

In What Ways Can You Apply This To Your Life?

_____
_____
_____
_____
_____

Who Could You Pray For Right Now Based On This Scripture?

_____
_____
_____
_____

JANUARY 16

"Go," said Jesus, "your faith has healed you."
Immediately he received his sight and followed
Jesus along the road. Mark 10:52

How Does This Scripture Speak To You?

_____

_____

_____

_____

_____

In What Ways Can You Apply This To Your Life?

_____

_____

_____

_____

_____

Who Could You Pray For Right Now Based On This Scripture?

_____

_____

_____

_____

JANUARY 17

If I have the gift of prophecy and can fathom all mysteries and all knowledge, and if I have a faith that can move mountains, but do not have love, I am nothing. 1 Corinthians 13:2

How Does This Scripture Speak To You?

_____
_____
_____
_____
_____

In What Ways Can You Apply This To Your Life?

_____
_____
_____
_____
_____

Who Could You Pray For Right Now Based On This Scripture?

_____
_____
_____
_____

JANUARY 18

Then Jesus declared, "I am the bread of life. Whoever comes to me will never go hungry, and whoever believes in me will never be thirsty."
John 6:35

How Does This Scripture Speak To You?

_____

_____

_____

_____

_____

In What Ways Can You Apply This To Your Life?

_____

_____

_____

_____

_____

Who Could You Pray For Right Now Based On This Scripture?

_____

_____

_____

_____

JANUARY 19

I have chosen the way of faithfulness;
I have set my heart on your laws.
Psalm 119:30

How Does This Scripture Speak To You?

_____

_____

_____

_____

_____

In What Ways Can You Apply This To Your Life?

_____

_____

_____

_____

_____

Who Could You Pray For Right Now Based On This Scripture?

_____

_____

_____

_____

JANUARY 20

If you believe, you will receive whatever
you ask for in prayer.
Matthew 21:22

How Does This Scripture Speak To You?

_____
_____
_____
_____
_____

In What Ways Can You Apply This To Your Life?

_____
_____
_____
_____
_____

Who Could You Pray For Right Now Based On This Scripture?

_____
_____
_____
_____

JANUARY 21

And by faith even Sarah, who was past childbearing age, was enabled to bear children because she considered him faithful who had made the promise.
Hebrews 11:11

How Does This Scripture Speak To You?

_____

_____

_____

_____

_____

In What Ways Can You Apply This To Your Life?

_____

_____

_____

_____

_____

Who Could You Pray For Right Now Based On This Scripture?

_____

_____

_____

_____

JANUARY 22

For it is with your heart that you believe and are justified, and it is with your mouth that you profess your faith and are saved.
Romans 10:10

How Does This Scripture Speak To You?

_____

_____

_____

_____

_____

In What Ways Can You Apply This To Your Life?

_____

_____

_____

_____

_____

Who Could You Pray For Right Now Based On This Scripture?

_____

_____

_____

_____

JANUARY 23

So in Christ Jesus you are all children of God through faith, for all of you who were baptized into Christ have clothed yourselves with Christ.
Galatians 3:26-27

How Does This Scripture Speak To You?

_____

_____

_____

_____

_____

In What Ways Can You Apply This To Your Life?

_____

_____

_____

_____

_____

Who Could You Pray For Right Now Based On This Scripture?

_____

_____

_____

_____

JANUARY 24

For in the gospel the righteousness of God is
revealed – a righteousness that is by faith from first
to last, just as it is written: "The righteous will live
by faith." Romans 1:17

How Does This Scripture Speak To You?

_____
_____
_____
_____
_____

In What Ways Can You Apply This To Your Life?

_____
_____
_____
_____
_____

Who Could You Pray For Right Now Based On This Scripture?

_____
_____
_____
_____

JANUARY 25

For God so loved the world that he gave his one and
only Son, that whoever believes in him shall not perish
but have eternal life.
John 3:16

How Does This Scripture Speak To You?

_____

_____

_____

_____

_____

In What Ways Can You Apply This To Your Life?

_____

_____

_____

_____

_____

Who Could You Pray For Right Now Based On This Scripture?

_____

_____

_____

_____

JANUARY 26

Whoever believes and is baptized will be saved, but whoever does not believe will be condemned.
Mark 16:16

How Does This Scripture Speak To You?

_____

_____

_____

_____

_____

In What Ways Can You Apply This To Your Life?

_____

_____

_____

_____

_____

Who Could You Pray For Right Now Based On This Scripture?

_____

_____

_____

_____

JANUARY 27

And now these three remain: faith, hope and love. But the greatest of these is love.
1 Corinthians 13:13

How Does This Scripture Speak To You?

_____
_____
_____
_____
_____

In What Ways Can You Apply This To Your Life?

_____
_____
_____
_____
_____

Who Could You Pray For Right Now Based On This Scripture?

_____
_____
_____
_____

JANUARY 28

They replied, "Believe in the Lord Jesus, and you will
be saved – you and your household."
Acts 16:31

How Does This Scripture Speak To You?

_____

_____

_____

_____

_____

In What Ways Can You Apply This To Your Life?

_____

_____

_____

_____

_____

Who Could You Pray For Right Now Based On This Scripture?

_____

_____

_____

_____

JANUARY 29

Be on your guard; stand firm in the faith;
be courageous; be strong.
1 Corinthians 16:13

How Does This Scripture Speak To You?

_____
_____
_____
_____
_____

In What Ways Can You Apply This To Your Life?

_____
_____
_____
_____
_____

Who Could You Pray For Right Now Based On This Scripture?

_____
_____
_____
_____

JANUARY 30

I write these things to you who believe in the
name of the Son of God so that you may
know that you have eternal life.
1 John 5:13

How Does This Scripture Speak To You?

_____

_____

_____

_____

_____

In What Ways Can You Apply This To Your Life?

_____

_____

_____

_____

_____

Who Could You Pray For Right Now Based On This Scripture?

_____

_____

_____

_____

JANUARY 31

In the same way, faith by itself, if it is not
accompanied by action, is dead.
James 2:17

How Does This Scripture Speak To You?

_____

_____

_____

_____

_____

In What Ways Can You Apply This To Your Life?

_____

_____

_____

_____

_____

**Who Could You Pray For Right Now Based On
This Scripture?**

_____

_____

_____

_____

February

Protection Scriptures

FEBRUARY 1

Put on the full armor of God, so that you can take your stand against the devil's schemes.
Ephesians 6:11

How Does This Scripture Speak To You?

_____
_____
_____
_____

In What Ways Can You Apply This To Your Life?

_____
_____
_____
_____

Who Could You Pray For Right Now Based On This Scripture?

_____
_____
_____

FEBRUARY 2

You are my hiding place;
you will protect me from trouble
and surround me with songs of deliverance.
Psalm 32:7

How Does This Scripture Speak To You?

_____
_____
_____
_____
_____

In What Ways Can You Apply This To Your Life?

_____
_____
_____
_____
_____

Who Could You Pray For Right Now Based On This Scripture?

_____
_____
_____
_____

FEBRUARY 3

God is our refuge and strength,
an ever-present help in trouble.
Psalm 46:1

How Does This Scripture Speak To You?

_____
_____
_____
_____
_____

In What Ways Can You Apply This To Your Life?

_____
_____
_____
_____
_____

Who Could You Pray For Right Now Based On This Scripture?

_____
_____
_____
_____

FEBRUARY 4

So we say with confidence,
"The Lord is my helper; I will not be afraid.
What can mere mortals do to me?"
Hebrews 13:6

How Does This Scripture Speak To You?

_____
_____
_____
_____
_____

In What Ways Can You Apply This To Your Life?

_____
_____
_____
_____
_____

Who Could You Pray For Right Now Based On This Scripture?

_____
_____
_____
_____

FEBRUARY 5

Be strong and courageous. Do not be afraid or terrified because of them, for the Lord your God goes with you; he will never leave you nor forsake you.
Deuteronomy 31:6

How Does This Scripture Speak To You?

_____

_____

_____

_____

_____

In What Ways Can You Apply This To Your Life?

_____

_____

_____

_____

_____

Who Could You Pray For Right Now Based On This Scripture?

_____

_____

_____

_____

FEBRUARY 6

"No weapon forged against you will prevail,
and you will refute every tongue that accuses you.
This is the heritage of the servants of the Lord,
and this is their vindication from me,"
declares the Lord. Isaiah 54:17

How Does This Scripture Speak To You?

_____

_____

_____

_____

_____

In What Ways Can You Apply This To Your Life?

_____

_____

_____

_____

_____

Who Could You Pray For Right Now Based On This Scripture?

_____

_____

_____

_____

FEBRUARY 7

You make your saving help my shield,
and your right hand sustains me;
your help has made me great.
You provide a broad path for my feet,
so that my ankles do not give way. Psalm 18:35-36

How Does This Scripture Speak To You?

_____
_____
_____
_____
_____

In What Ways Can You Apply This To Your Life?

_____
_____
_____
_____
_____

Who Could You Pray For Right Now Based On This Scripture?

_____
_____
_____
_____

FEBRUARY 8

Keep me safe, my God,
for in you I take refuge.
<u>Psalm 16:1</u>

How Does This Scripture Speak To You?

_____
_____
_____
_____
_____

In What Ways Can You Apply This To Your Life?

_____
_____
_____
_____
_____

Who Could You Pray For Right Now Based On This Scripture?

_____
_____
_____
_____

FEBRUARY 9

The Lord will fight for you; you need only to be still.
Exodus 14:14

How Does This Scripture Speak To You?

_____
_____
_____
_____
_____

In What Ways Can You Apply This To Your Life?

_____
_____
_____
_____
_____

**Who Could You Pray For Right Now Based On
This Scripture?**

_____
_____
_____
_____

FEBRUARY 10

The Lord is with me; I will not be afraid.
What can mere mortals do to me?
Psalm 118:6

How Does This Scripture Speak To You?

_____

_____

_____

_____

_____

In What Ways Can You Apply This To Your Life?

_____

_____

_____

_____

_____

Who Could You Pray For Right Now Based On This Scripture?

_____

_____

_____

_____

FEBRUARY 11

I can do all this through him who gives me strength.
Philippians 4:13

How Does This Scripture Speak To You?

_____

_____

_____

_____

_____

In What Ways Can You Apply This To Your Life?

_____

_____

_____

_____

_____

Who Could You Pray For Right Now Based On This Scripture?

_____

_____

_____

_____

FEBRUARY 12

You are my refuge and my shield;
I have put my hope in your word.
Psalm 119:114

How Does This Scripture Speak To You?

_____
_____
_____
_____
_____

In What Ways Can You Apply This To Your Life?

_____
_____
_____
_____
_____

Who Could You Pray For Right Now Based On This Scripture?

_____
_____
_____
_____

FEBRUARY 13

Even to your old age and gray hairs
I am he, I am he who will sustain you.
I have made you and I will carry you;
I will sustain you and I will rescue you.
Isaiah 46:4

How Does This Scripture Speak To You?

_____
_____
_____
_____
_____

In What Ways Can You Apply This To Your Life?

_____
_____
_____
_____
_____

Who Could You Pray For Right Now Based On This Scripture?

_____
_____
_____
_____

FEBRUARY 14

Above all else, guard your heart,
for everything you do flows from it.
Proverbs 4:23

How Does This Scripture Speak To You?

_____

_____

_____

_____

_____

In What Ways Can You Apply This To Your Life?

_____

_____

_____

_____

_____

Who Could You Pray For Right Now Based On This Scripture?

_____

_____

_____

_____

FEBRUARY 15

As for God, his way is perfect:
The Lord's word is flawless;
he shields all who take refuge in him.
Psalm 18:30

How Does This Scripture Speak To You?

_____
_____
_____
_____
_____

In What Ways Can You Apply This To Your Life?

_____
_____
_____
_____
_____

Who Could You Pray For Right Now Based On This Scripture?

_____
_____
_____
_____

FEBRUARY 16

I keep my eyes always on the Lord.
With him at my right hand, I will not be shaken.
Psalm 16:8

How Does This Scripture Speak To You?

_____
_____
_____
_____
_____

In What Ways Can You Apply This To Your Life?

_____
_____
_____
_____
_____

Who Could You Pray For Right Now Based On This Scripture?

_____
_____
_____
_____

FEBRUARY 17

But I will sing of your strength,
in the morning I will sing of your love;
for you are my fortress,
my refuge in times of trouble.
Psalm 59:16

How Does This Scripture Speak To You?

_____
_____
_____
_____
_____

In What Ways Can You Apply This To Your Life?

_____
_____
_____
_____
_____

**Who Could You Pray For Right Now Based On
This Scripture?**

_____
_____
_____
_____

FEBRUARY 18

But you, Lord, are a shield around me,
my glory, the One who lifts my head high.
<u>Psalm 3:3</u>

How Does This Scripture Speak To You?

_____

_____

_____

_____

_____

In What Ways Can You Apply This To Your Life?

_____

_____

_____

_____

_____

Who Could You Pray For Right Now Based On This Scripture?

_____

_____

_____

_____

FEBRUARY 19

What, then, shall we say in response to these things? If
God is for us, who can be against us?
Romans 8:31

How Does This Scripture Speak To You?

_____
_____
_____
_____
_____

In What Ways Can You Apply This To Your Life?

_____
_____
_____
_____
_____

Who Could You Pray For Right Now Based On This Scripture?

_____
_____
_____
_____

FEBRUARY 20

It is better to take refuge in the Lord
than to trust in humans.
Psalm 118:8

How Does This Scripture Speak To You?

_____
_____
_____
_____
_____

In What Ways Can You Apply This To Your Life?

_____
_____
_____
_____
_____

Who Could You Pray For Right Now Based On This Scripture?

_____
_____
_____
_____

FEBRUARY 21

Every word of God is flawless;
he is a shield to those who take refuge in him.
Proverbs 30:5

How Does This Scripture Speak To You?

_____
_____
_____
_____
_____

In What Ways Can You Apply This To Your Life?

_____
_____
_____
_____
_____

Who Could You Pray For Right Now Based On This Scripture?

_____
_____
_____
_____

FEBRUARY 22

The name of the Lord is a fortified tower;
the righteous run to it and are safe.
Proverbs 18:10

How Does This Scripture Speak To You?

_____

_____

_____

_____

_____

In What Ways Can You Apply This To Your Life?

_____

_____

_____

_____

_____

Who Could You Pray For Right Now Based On This Scripture?

_____

_____

_____

_____

FEBRUARY 23

The Lord will rescue his servants;
no one who takes refuge in him will be condemned.
Psalm 34:22

How Does This Scripture Speak To You?

_____
_____
_____
_____
_____

In What Ways Can You Apply This To Your Life?

_____
_____
_____
_____
_____

**Who Could You Pray For Right Now Based On
This Scripture?**

_____
_____
_____
_____

FEBRUARY 24

Learn to do right; seek justice.
Defend the oppressed.
Take up the cause of the fatherless;
plead the case of the widow.
Isaiah 1:17

How Does This Scripture Speak To You?

_____

_____

_____

_____

_____

In What Ways Can You Apply This To Your Life?

_____

_____

_____

_____

_____

Who Could You Pray For Right Now Based On This Scripture?

_____

_____

_____

FEBRUARY 25

For who is God besides the Lord?
And who is the Rock except our God?
2 Samuel 22:32

How Does This Scripture Speak To You?

_____

_____

_____

_____

_____

In What Ways Can You Apply This To Your Life?

_____

_____

_____

_____

_____

Who Could You Pray For Right Now Based On This Scripture?

_____

_____

_____

_____

FEBRUARY 26

Do you think I cannot call on my Father, and
he will at once put at my disposal more than
twelve legions of angels?
Matthew 26:53

How Does This Scripture Speak To You?

_____

_____

_____

_____

_____

In What Ways Can You Apply This To Your Life?

_____

_____

_____

_____

_____

Who Could You Pray For Right Now Based On This Scripture?

_____

_____

_____

_____

FEBRUARY 27

He will cover you with his feathers,
and under his wings you will find refuge;
his faithfulness will be your shield and rampart.
Psalm 91:4

How Does This Scripture Speak To You?

_____

_____

_____

_____

_____

In What Ways Can You Apply This To Your Life?

_____

_____

_____

_____

_____

Who Could You Pray For Right Now Based On This Scripture?

_____

_____

_____

_____

FEBRUARY 28

The Lord is good,
a refuge in times of trouble.
He cares for those who trust in him.
Nahum 1:7

How Does This Scripture Speak To You?

_____
_____
_____
_____
_____

In What Ways Can You Apply This To Your Life?

_____
_____
_____
_____
_____

Who Could You Pray For Right Now Based On This Scripture?

_____
_____
_____
_____

March

Relationship Scriptures

MARCH 1

Greater love has no one than this: to lay
down one's life for one's friends.
John 15:13

How Does This Scripture Speak To You?

_____

_____

_____

_____

_____

In What Ways Can You Apply This To Your Life?

_____

_____

_____

_____

_____

**Who Could You Pray For Right Now Based On
This Scripture?**

_____

_____

_____

_____

MARCH 2

A friend loves at all times,
and a brother is born for a time of adversity.
Proverbs 17:17

How Does This Scripture Speak To You?

_____

_____

_____

_____

_____

In What Ways Can You Apply This To Your Life?

_____

_____

_____

_____

_____

Who Could You Pray For Right Now Based On This Scripture?

_____

_____

_____

_____

MARCH 3

One who has unreliable friends soon comes to ruin,
but there is a friend who sticks closer than a brother.
Proverbs 18:24

How Does This Scripture Speak To You?

_____
_____
_____
_____
_____

In What Ways Can You Apply This To Your Life?

_____
_____
_____
_____
_____

Who Could You Pray For Right Now Based On This Scripture?

_____
_____
_____
_____

MARCH 4

Whoever would foster love covers over an offense,
but whoever repeats the matter separates close friends.
Proverbs 17:9

How Does This Scripture Speak To You?

_____
_____
_____
_____
_____

In What Ways Can You Apply This To Your Life?

_____
_____
_____
_____
_____

Who Could You Pray For Right Now Based On This Scripture?

_____
_____
_____
_____

MARCH 5

How good and pleasant it is
when God's people live together in unity!
Psalm 133:1

How Does This Scripture Speak To You?

_____
_____
_____
_____
_____

In What Ways Can You Apply This To Your Life?

_____
_____
_____
_____
_____

Who Could You Pray For Right Now Based On This Scripture?

_____
_____
_____

MARCH 6

Dear friends, let us love one another, for love comes from God. Everyone who loves has been born of God and knows God.
1 John 4:7

How Does This Scripture Speak To You?

_____

_____

_____

_____

_____

In What Ways Can You Apply This To Your Life?

_____

_____

_____

_____

Who Could You Pray For Right Now Based On This Scripture?

_____

_____

_____

_____

MARCH 7

A perverse person stirs up conflict,
and a gossip separates close friends.
Proverbs 16:28

How Does This Scripture Speak To You?

_____
_____
_____
_____
_____

In What Ways Can You Apply This To Your Life?

_____
_____
_____
_____
_____

Who Could You Pray For Right Now Based On This Scripture?

_____
_____
_____
_____

MARCH 8

Anyone who withholds kindness from a friend
forsakes the fear of the Almighty.
<u>Job 6:14</u>

How Does This Scripture Speak To You?

_____
_____
_____
_____
_____

In What Ways Can You Apply This To Your Life?

_____
_____
_____
_____
_____

Who Could You Pray For Right Now Based On This Scripture?

_____
_____
_____
_____

MARCH 9

And he has given us this command: Anyone who loves
God must also love their brother and sister.
1 John 4:21

How Does This Scripture Speak To You?

_____
_____
_____
_____
_____

In What Ways Can You Apply This To Your Life?

_____
_____
_____
_____
_____

Who Could You Pray For Right Now Based On This Scripture?

_____
_____
_____
_____

MARCH 10

As iron sharpens iron,
so one person sharpens another.
Proverbs 27:17

How Does This Scripture Speak To You?

_____

_____

_____

_____

_____

In What Ways Can You Apply This To Your Life?

_____

_____

_____

_____

_____

Who Could You Pray For Right Now Based On This Scripture?

_____

_____

_____

_____

MARCH 11

Though one may be overpowered,
two can defend themselves.
A cord of three strands is not quickly broken.
Ecclesiastes 4:12

How Does This Scripture Speak To You?

_____
_____
_____
_____
_____

In What Ways Can You Apply This To Your Life?

_____
_____
_____
_____
_____

Who Could You Pray For Right Now Based On This Scripture?

_____
_____
_____
_____

MARCH 12

If either of them falls down,
one can help the other up.
But pity anyone who falls
and has no one to help them up.
Ecclesiastes 4:10

How Does This Scripture Speak To You?

_____
_____
_____
_____
_____

In What Ways Can You Apply This To Your Life?

_____
_____
_____
_____
_____

Who Could You Pray For Right Now Based On This Scripture?

_____
_____
_____

MARCH 13

You adulterous people, don't you know that friendship with the world means enmity against God? Therefore, anyone who chooses to be a friend of the world becomes an enemy of God.
James 4:4

How Does This Scripture Speak To You?

_____
_____
_____
_____
_____

In What Ways Can You Apply This To Your Life?

_____
_____
_____
_____
_____

Who Could You Pray For Right Now Based On This Scripture?

_____
_____
_____
_____

MARCH 14

Two are better than one,
because they have a good return for their labor.
Ecclesiastes 4:9

How Does This Scripture Speak To You?

_____

_____

_____

_____

_____

In What Ways Can You Apply This To Your Life?

_____

_____

_____

_____

_____

Who Could You Pray For Right Now Based On This Scripture?

_____

_____

_____

_____

MARCH 15

Do not be misled: "Bad company corrupts good character."
1 Corinthians 15:33

How Does This Scripture Speak To You?

_____

_____

_____

_____

_____

In What Ways Can You Apply This To Your Life?

_____

_____

_____

_____

_____

Who Could You Pray For Right Now Based On This Scripture?

_____

_____

_____

_____

MARCH 16

Do not forsake your friend or a friend of your family, and do not go to your relative's house when disaster strikes you – better a neighbor nearby than a relative far away.

Proverbs 27:10

How Does This Scripture Speak To You?

_____

_____

_____

_____

_____

In What Ways Can You Apply This To Your Life?

_____

_____

_____

_____

_____

Who Could You Pray For Right Now Based On This Scripture?

_____

_____

_____

_____

MARCH 17

I long to see you so that I may impart to you some spiritual gift to make you strong— that is, that you and I may be mutually encouraged by each other's faith.
Romans 1:11-12

How Does This Scripture Speak To You?

_____
_____
_____
_____
_____

In What Ways Can You Apply This To Your Life?

_____
_____
_____
_____
_____

Who Could You Pray For Right Now Based On This Scripture?

_____
_____
_____
_____

MARCH 18

'Honor your father and mother,' and 'love your
neighbor as yourself.'
Matthew 19:19

How Does This Scripture Speak To You?

_____

_____

_____

_____

_____

In What Ways Can You Apply This To Your Life?

_____

_____

_____

_____

_____

Who Could You Pray For Right Now Based On This Scripture?

_____

_____

_____

_____

MARCH 19

God sets the lonely in families,
he leads out the prisoners with singing;
but the rebellious live in a sun-scorched land.
Psalm 68:6

How Does This Scripture Speak To You?

_____
_____
_____
_____

In What Ways Can You Apply This To Your Life?

_____
_____
_____
_____

Who Could You Pray For Right Now Based On This Scripture?

_____
_____
_____
_____

MARCH 20

A wife of noble character who can find?
She is worth far more than rubies.
Proverbs 31:10

How Does This Scripture Speak To You?

_____
_____
_____
_____
_____

In What Ways Can You Apply This To Your Life?

_____
_____
_____
_____
_____

Who Could You Pray For Right Now Based On This Scripture?

_____
_____
_____

MARCH 21

Husbands love your wives, just as Christ loved the church and gave himself up for her to make her holy, cleansing her by the washing with water through the word.
Ephesians 5:25-26

How Does This Scripture Speak To You?

_____

_____

_____

_____

_____

In What Ways Can You Apply This To Your Life?

_____

_____

_____

_____

_____

Who Could You Pray For Right Now Based On This Scripture?

_____

_____

_____

_____

MARCH 22

Wives, submit yourselves to your husbands, as is
fitting in the Lord. Husbands love your wives and
do not be harsh with them.
Colossians 3:18-19

How Does This Scripture Speak To You?

_____

_____

_____

_____

_____

In What Ways Can You Apply This To Your Life?

_____

_____

_____

_____

_____

Who Could You Pray For Right Now Based On This Scripture?

_____

_____

_____

_____

MARCH 23

So in everything, do to others what you would have them do to you, for this sums up the Law and the Prophets.
Matthew 7:12

How Does This Scripture Speak To You?

_____
_____
_____
_____
_____

In What Ways Can You Apply This To Your Life?

_____
_____
_____
_____
_____

Who Could You Pray For Right Now Based On This Scripture?

_____
_____
_____
_____

MARCH 24

For this very reason, make every effort to add to your faith goodness; and to goodness, knowledge; and to knowledge, self-control; and to self-control, perseverance; and to perseverance, godliness; and to godliness, mutual affection; and to mutual affection, love.

2 Peter 1:5-7

How Does This Scripture Speak To You?

_____

_____

_____

_____

_____

In What Ways Can You Apply This To Your Life?

_____

_____

_____

_____

_____

Who Could You Pray For Right Now Based On This Scripture?

_____

_____

_____

_____

MARCH 25

The Lord God said, "It is not good for the man to be alone. I will make a helper suitable for him."
Genesis 2:18

How Does This Scripture Speak To You?

_____

_____

_____

_____

_____

In What Ways Can You Apply This To Your Life?

_____

_____

_____

_____

_____

Who Could You Pray For Right Now Based On This Scripture?

_____

_____

_____

_____

MARCH 26

Do not be yoked together with unbelievers. For what do righteousness and wickedness have in common? Or what fellowship can light have with darkness?
2 Corinthians 6:14

How Does This Scripture Speak To You?

_____

_____

_____

_____

_____

In What Ways Can You Apply This To Your Life?

_____

_____

_____

_____

Who Could You Pray For Right Now Based On This Scripture?

_____

_____

_____

MARCH 27

But since sexual immorality is occurring, each man should have sexual relations with his own wife, and each woman with her own husband.
<u>1 Corinthians 7:2</u>

How Does This Scripture Speak To You?

_____
_____
_____
_____
_____

In What Ways Can You Apply This To Your Life?

_____
_____
_____
_____
_____

Who Could You Pray For Right Now Based On This Scripture?

_____
_____
_____
_____

MARCH 28

Houses and wealth are inherited from parents,
but a prudent wife is from the Lord.
Proverbs 19:14

How Does This Scripture Speak To You?

_____
_____
_____
_____
_____

In What Ways Can You Apply This To Your Life?

_____
_____
_____
_____
_____

Who Could You Pray For Right Now Based On This Scripture?

_____
_____
_____
_____

MARCH 29

Two are better than one,
because they have a good return for their labor.
Ecclesiastes 4:9

How Does This Scripture Speak To You?

_____

_____

_____

_____

_____

In What Ways Can You Apply This To Your Life?

_____

_____

_____

_____

_____

Who Could You Pray For Right Now Based On This Scripture?

_____

_____

_____

_____

MARCH 30

If either of them falls down,
one can help the other up.
But pity anyone who falls
and has no one to help them up.
Ecclesiastes 4:10

How Does This Scripture Speak To You?

_____

_____

_____

_____

_____

In What Ways Can You Apply This To Your Life?

_____

_____

_____

_____

_____

Who Could You Pray For Right Now Based On This Scripture?

_____

_____

_____

_____

MARCH 31

May the Lord make your love increase and overflow for each other and for everyone else, just as ours does for you.
1 Thessalonians 3:12

How Does This Scripture Speak To You?

_____
_____
_____
_____
_____

In What Ways Can You Apply This To Your Life?

_____
_____
_____
_____
_____

Who Could You Pray For Right Now Based On This Scripture?

_____
_____
_____
_____

April

Peace Scriptures

APRIL 1

"The Lord bless you and keep you;
the Lord make his face shine on you
and be gracious to you;
the Lord turn his face toward you and give you peace."
Numbers 6:24-26

How Does This Scripture Speak To You?

_____

_____

_____

_____

_____

In What Ways Can You Apply This To Your Life?

_____

_____

_____

_____

_____

Who Could You Pray For Right Now Based On This Scripture?

_____

_____

_____

_____

APRIL 2

I have told you these things, so that in me you may
have peace. In this world you will have trouble. But
take heart! I have overcome the world.
John 16:33

How Does This Scripture Speak To You?

_____
_____
_____
_____
_____

In What Ways Can You Apply This To Your Life?

_____
_____
_____
_____
_____

Who Could You Pray For Right Now Based On This Scripture?

_____
_____
_____
_____

APRIL 3

Peace I leave with you; my peace I give you. I do not give to you as the world gives. Do not let your hearts be troubled and do not be afraid.
John 14:27

How Does This Scripture Speak To You?

_____
_____
_____
_____
_____

In What Ways Can You Apply This To Your Life?

_____
_____
_____
_____
_____

Who Could You Pray For Right Now Based On This Scripture?

_____
_____
_____

APRIL 4

Blessed are the peacemakers,
for they will be called children of God.
Matthew 5:9

How Does This Scripture Speak To You?

_____
_____
_____
_____
_____

In What Ways Can You Apply This To Your Life?

_____
_____
_____
_____
_____

Who Could You Pray For Right Now Based On This Scripture?

_____
_____
_____
_____

APRIL 5

For, Whoever would love life and see good days must keep their tongue from evil and their lips from deceitful speech. They must turn from evil and do good; they must seek peace and pursue it.
1 Peter 3:10-11

How Does This Scripture Speak To You?

_____

_____

_____

_____

_____

In What Ways Can You Apply This To Your Life?

_____

_____

_____

_____

Who Could You Pray For Right Now Based On This Scripture?

_____

_____

_____

_____

APRIL 6

Do not be anxious about anything, but in every situation, by prayer and petition, with thanksgiving, present your requests to God. And the peace of God, which transcends all understanding, will guard your hearts and your minds in Christ Jesus. Philippians 4:6-7

How Does This Scripture Speak To You?

_____

_____

_____

_____

_____

In What Ways Can You Apply This To Your Life?

_____

_____

_____

_____

_____

Who Could You Pray For Right Now Based On This Scripture?

_____

_____

_____

_____

APRIL 7

In peace I will lie down and sleep,
for you alone, Lord,
make me dwell in safety.
Psalm 4:8

How Does This Scripture Speak To You?

_____
_____
_____
_____
_____

In What Ways Can You Apply This To Your Life?

_____
_____
_____
_____
_____

Who Could You Pray For Right Now Based On This Scripture?

_____
_____
_____
_____

APRIL 8

Bear with each other and forgive one another if any of you has a grievance against someone. Forgive as the Lord forgave you.
Colossians 3:13

How Does This Scripture Speak To You?

_____
_____
_____
_____
_____

In What Ways Can You Apply This To Your Life?

_____
_____
_____
_____
_____

Who Could You Pray For Right Now Based On This Scripture?

_____
_____
_____
_____

APRIL 9

Now may the Lord of peace himself give you peace at all times and in every way. The Lord be with all of you.
2 Thessalonians 3:16

How Does This Scripture Speak To You?

_____
_____
_____
_____
_____

In What Ways Can You Apply This To Your Life?

_____
_____
_____
_____
_____

Who Could You Pray For Right Now Based On This Scripture?

_____
_____
_____
_____

APRIL 10

Let the peace of Christ rule in your hearts, since as
members of one body you were called to peace.
And be thankful.
Colossians 3:15

How Does This Scripture Speak To You?

_____
_____
_____
_____
_____

In What Ways Can You Apply This To Your Life?

_____
_____
_____
_____
_____

Who Could You Pray For Right Now Based On This Scripture?

_____
_____
_____
_____

APRIL 11

You will keep in perfect peace
those whose minds are steadfast,
because they trust in you.
Isaiah 26:3

How Does This Scripture Speak To You?

_____
_____
_____
_____
_____

In What Ways Can You Apply This To Your Life?

_____
_____
_____
_____
_____

Who Could You Pray For Right Now Based On This Scripture?

_____
_____
_____
_____

APRIL 12

Better a patient person than a warrior,
one with self-control than one who takes a city.
Proverbs 16:32

How Does This Scripture Speak To You?

_____

_____

_____

_____

_____

In What Ways Can You Apply This To Your Life?

_____

_____

_____

_____

_____

Who Could You Pray For Right Now Based On This Scripture?

_____

_____

_____

_____

APRIL 13

Peacemakers who sow in peace reap a harvest of
righteousness.
James 3:18

How Does This Scripture Speak To You?

_____

_____

_____

_____

_____

In What Ways Can You Apply This To Your Life?

_____

_____

_____

_____

_____

Who Could You Pray For Right Now Based On This Scripture?

_____

_____

_____

_____

APRIL 14

Mercy, peace and love be yours in abundance.
Jude 1:2

How Does This Scripture Speak To You?

_____
_____
_____
_____
_____

In What Ways Can You Apply This To Your Life?

_____
_____
_____
_____
_____

Who Could You Pray For Right Now Based On This Scripture?

_____
_____
_____
_____

APRIL 15

Make every effort to live in peace with everyone and to be holy; without holiness no one will see the Lord.
Hebrews 12:14

How Does This Scripture Speak To You?

_____

_____

_____

_____

_____

In What Ways Can You Apply This To Your Life?

_____

_____

_____

_____

_____

Who Could You Pray For Right Now Based On This Scripture?

_____

_____

_____

_____

APRIL 16

Turn from evil and do good;
seek peace and pursue it.
Psalm 34:14

How Does This Scripture Speak To You?

_____
_____
_____
_____
_____

In What Ways Can You Apply This To Your Life?

_____
_____
_____
_____
_____

Who Could You Pray For Right Now Based On This Scripture?

_____
_____
_____
_____

APRIL 17

Make every effort to keep the unity of the Spirit
through the bond of peace.
Ephesians 4:3

How Does This Scripture Speak To You?

_____

_____

_____

_____

_____

In What Ways Can You Apply This To Your Life?

_____

_____

_____

_____

_____

Who Could You Pray For Right Now Based On This Scripture?

_____

_____

_____

_____

APRIL 18

But the wisdom that comes from heaven is first of all pure; then peace-loving, considerate, submissive, full of mercy and good fruit, impartial and sincere.
James 3:17

How Does This Scripture Speak To You?

_____

_____

_____

_____

_____

In What Ways Can You Apply This To Your Life?

_____

_____

_____

_____

_____

Who Could You Pray For Right Now Based On This Scripture?

_____

_____

_____

_____

APRIL 19

Whatever you have learned or received or heard from me, or seen in me—put it into practice. And the God of peace will be with you.
<u>Philippians 4:9</u>

How Does This Scripture Speak To You?

_____
_____
_____
_____
_____

In What Ways Can You Apply This To Your Life?

_____
_____
_____
_____
_____

Who Could You Pray For Right Now Based On This Scripture?

_____
_____
_____
_____

APRIL 20

Great peace have those who love your law,
and nothing can make them stumble.
Psalm 119:165

How Does This Scripture Speak To You?

_____
_____
_____
_____
_____

In What Ways Can You Apply This To Your Life?

_____
_____
_____
_____
_____

Who Could You Pray For Right Now Based On This Scripture?

_____
_____
_____
_____

APRIL 21

The mind governed by the flesh is death, but the mind governed by the Spirit is life and peace.
Romans 8:6

How Does This Scripture Speak To You?

_____
_____
_____
_____
_____

In What Ways Can You Apply This To Your Life?

_____
_____
_____
_____

Who Could You Pray For Right Now Based On This Scripture?

_____
_____
_____
_____

APRIL 22

How beautiful on the mountains are the feet of those
who bring good news, who proclaim peace,
who bring good tidings, who proclaim salvation,
who say to Zion, "Your God reigns!"
Isaiah 52:7

How Does This Scripture Speak To You?

_____

_____

_____

_____

_____

In What Ways Can You Apply This To Your Life?

_____

_____

_____

_____

_____

**Who Could You Pray For Right Now Based On
This Scripture?**

_____

_____

_____

_____

APRIL 23

It is to one's honor to avoid strife,
but every fool is quick to quarrel.
<u>Proverbs 20:3</u>

How Does This Scripture Speak To You?

_____
_____
_____
_____
_____

In What Ways Can You Apply This To Your Life?

_____
_____
_____
_____
_____

Who Could You Pray For Right Now Based On This Scripture?

_____
_____
_____
_____

APRIL 24

No discipline seems pleasant at the time, but painful.
Later on, however, it produces a harvest of
righteousness and peace for those who have been
trained by it.
Hebrews 12:11

How Does This Scripture Speak To You?

_____

_____

_____

_____

In What Ways Can You Apply This To Your Life?

_____

_____

_____

_____

**Who Could You Pray For Right Now Based On
This Scripture?**

_____

_____

_____

_____

APRIL 25

He says, "Be still, and know that I am God;
I will be exalted among the nations,
I will be exalted in the earth."
Psalm 46:10

How Does This Scripture Speak To You?

_____
_____
_____
_____
_____

In What Ways Can You Apply This To Your Life?

_____
_____
_____
_____
_____

Who Could You Pray For Right Now Based On This Scripture?

_____
_____
_____
_____

APRIL 26

Therefore, since we have been justified through faith, we have peace with God through our Lord Jesus Christ.
Romans 5:1

How Does This Scripture Speak To You?

_____

_____

_____

_____

_____

In What Ways Can You Apply This To Your Life?

_____

_____

_____

_____

_____

Who Could You Pray For Right Now Based On This Scripture?

_____

_____

_____

_____

APRIL 27

"Glory to God in the highest heaven,
and on earth peace to those on whom his favor rests."
Luke 2:14

How Does This Scripture Speak To You?

_____

_____

_____

_____

_____

In What Ways Can You Apply This To Your Life?

_____

_____

_____

_____

_____

Who Could You Pray For Right Now Based On This Scripture?

_____

_____

_____

_____

APRIL 28

The Lord gives strength to his people;
the Lord blesses his people with peace.
Psalm 29:11

How Does This Scripture Speak To You?

_____
_____
_____
_____
_____

In What Ways Can You Apply This To Your Life?

_____
_____
_____
_____
_____

Who Could You Pray For Right Now Based On This Scripture?

_____
_____
_____
_____

APRIL 29

My son, do not forget my teaching,
but keep my commands in your heart,
for they will prolong your life many years
and bring you peace and prosperity.
<u>Proverbs 3:1-2</u>

How Does This Scripture Speak To You?

_____
_____
_____
_____
_____

In What Ways Can You Apply This To Your Life?

_____
_____
_____
_____
_____

Who Could You Pray For Right Now Based On This Scripture?

_____
_____
_____
_____

APRIL 30

Finally, brothers and sisters, rejoice! Strive for full restoration, encourage one another, be of one mind, live in peace. And the God of love and peace will be with you.
2 Corinthians 13:11

How Does This Scripture Speak To You?

_____

_____

_____

_____

_____

In What Ways Can You Apply This To Your Life?

_____

_____

_____

_____

_____

Who Could You Pray For Right Now Based On This Scripture?

_____

_____

_____

_____

May

Obedience Scriptures

MAY 1

Jesus replied, "Anyone who loves me will obey my
teaching. My Father will love them, and we will come
to them and make our home with them."
John 14:23

How Does This Scripture Speak To You?

_____

_____

_____

_____

_____

In What Ways Can You Apply This To Your Life?

_____

_____

_____

_____

Who Could You Pray For Right Now Based On
This Scripture?

_____

_____

_____

_____

MAY 2

My son, keep your father's command
and do not forsake your mother's teaching.
Proverbs 6:20

How Does This Scripture Speak To You?

_____

_____

_____

_____

_____

In What Ways Can You Apply This To Your Life?

_____

_____

_____

_____

_____

Who Could You Pray For Right Now Based On This Scripture?

_____

_____

_____

_____

MAY 3

If you fully obey the Lord your God and carefully follow all his commands I give you today, the Lord your God will set you high above all the nations on earth.
Deuteronomy 28:1

How Does This Scripture Speak To You?

_____
_____
_____
_____
_____

In What Ways Can You Apply This To Your Life?

_____
_____
_____
_____
_____

Who Could You Pray For Right Now Based On This Scripture?

_____
_____
_____

MAY 4

Walk in obedience to all that the Lord your God has commanded you, so that you may live and prosper and prolong your days in the land that you will possess.
Deuteronomy 5:33

How Does This Scripture Speak To You?

_____
_____
_____
_____
_____

In What Ways Can You Apply This To Your Life?

_____
_____
_____
_____
_____

Who Could You Pray For Right Now Based On This Scripture?

_____
_____
_____
_____

MAY 5

Do not merely listen to the word, and so deceive
yourselves. Do what it says.
James 1:22

How Does This Scripture Speak To You?

_____

_____

_____

_____

_____

In What Ways Can You Apply This To Your Life?

_____

_____

_____

_____

_____

Who Could You Pray For Right Now Based On This Scripture?

_____

_____

_____

_____

MAY 6

Whoever heeds discipline shows the way to life,
but whoever ignores correction leads others astray.
Proverbs 10:17

How Does This Scripture Speak To You?

_____
_____
_____
_____
_____

In What Ways Can You Apply This To Your Life?

_____
_____
_____
_____
_____

Who Could You Pray For Right Now Based On This Scripture?

_____
_____
_____
_____

MAY 7

You did not choose me, but I chose you and appointed
you so that you might go and bear fruit—fruit that
will last—and so that whatever you ask in my
name the Father will give you.
<u>John 15:16</u>

How Does This Scripture Speak To You?

_____

_____

_____

_____

_____

In What Ways Can You Apply This To Your Life?

_____

_____

_____

_____

_____

Who Could You Pray For Right Now Based On This Scripture?

_____

_____

_____

_____

MAY 8

Therefore, my dear brothers and sisters, stand firm. Let nothing move you. Always give yourselves fully to the work of the Lord, because you know that your labor in the Lord is not in vain.

1 Corinthians 15:58

How Does This Scripture Speak To You?

_____

_____

_____

_____

_____

In What Ways Can You Apply This To Your Life?

_____

_____

_____

_____

_____

Who Could You Pray For Right Now Based On This Scripture?

_____

_____

_____

_____

MAY 9

Do not conform to the pattern of this world, but be transformed by the renewing of your mind. Then you will be able to test and approve what God's will is—his good, pleasing and perfect will.
Romans 12:2

How Does This Scripture Speak To You?

_____
_____
_____
_____
_____

In What Ways Can You Apply This To Your Life?

_____
_____
_____
_____
_____

Who Could You Pray For Right Now Based On This Scripture?

_____
_____
_____
_____

MAY 10

Dear friends, if our hearts do not condemn us, we have confidence before God and receive from him anything we ask, because we keep his commands and do what pleases him.
1 John 3:21-22

How Does This Scripture Speak To You?

_____

_____

_____

_____

_____

In What Ways Can You Apply This To Your Life?

_____

_____

_____

_____

_____

Who Could You Pray For Right Now Based On This Scripture?

_____

_____

_____

_____

MAY 11

But to you who are listening I say: Love your enemies,
do good to those who hate you, bless those who
curse you, pray for those who mistreat you.
Luke 6:27-28

How Does This Scripture Speak To You?

_____
_____
_____
_____
_____

In What Ways Can You Apply This To Your Life?

_____
_____
_____
_____
_____

Who Could You Pray For Right Now Based On This Scripture?

_____
_____
_____
_____

MAY 12

For just as through the disobedience of the one man
the many were made sinners, so also through the
obedience of the one man the many will be made
righteous.
Romans 5:19

How Does This Scripture Speak To You?

_____

_____

_____

_____

_____

In What Ways Can You Apply This To Your Life?

_____

_____

_____

_____

_____

Who Could You Pray For Right Now Based On This Scripture?

_____

_____

_____

_____

MAY 13

Observe what the Lord your God requires: Walk in obedience to him, and keep his decrees and commands, his laws and regulations, as written in the Law of Moses. Do this so that you may prosper in all you do and wherever you go. 1 Kings 2:3

How Does This Scripture Speak To You?

_____

_____

_____

_____

_____

In What Ways Can You Apply This To Your Life?

_____

_____

_____

_____

Who Could You Pray For Right Now Based On This Scripture?

_____

_____

_____

_____

MAY 14

Keep this Book of the Law always on your lips; meditate on it day and night, so that you may be careful to do everything written in it. Then you will be prosperous and successful.

<u>Joshua 1:8</u>

How Does This Scripture Speak To You?

_____
_____
_____
_____
_____

In What Ways Can You Apply This To Your Life?

_____
_____
_____
_____
_____

Who Could You Pray For Right Now Based On This Scripture?

_____
_____
_____
_____

MAY 15

Submit yourselves, then, to God. Resist the devil, and
he will flee from you.
James 4:7

How Does This Scripture Speak To You?

_____

_____

_____

_____

_____

In What Ways Can You Apply This To Your Life?

_____

_____

_____

_____

_____

Who Could You Pray For Right Now Based On This Scripture?

_____

_____

_____

_____

MAY 16

"If you do not listen, and if you do not resolve to honor my name," says the Lord Almighty, "I will send a curse on you, and I will curse your blessings. Yes, I have already cursed them, because you have not resolved to honor me." Malachi 2:2

How Does This Scripture Speak To You?

_____
_____
_____
_____
_____

In What Ways Can You Apply This To Your Life?

_____
_____
_____
_____
_____

Who Could You Pray For Right Now Based On This Scripture?

_____
_____
_____
_____

MAY 17

Let everyone be subject to the governing authorities,
for there is no authority except that which God has
established. The authorities that exist have been
established by God.
Romans 13:1

How Does This Scripture Speak To You?

_____

_____

_____

_____

_____

In What Ways Can You Apply This To Your Life?

_____

_____

_____

_____

_____

Who Could You Pray For Right Now Based On This Scripture?

_____

_____

_____

_____

MAY 18

Never be lacking in zeal, but keep your spiritual fervor,
serving the Lord.
Romans 12:11

How Does This Scripture Speak To You?

_____

_____

_____

_____

_____

In What Ways Can You Apply This To Your Life?

_____

_____

_____

_____

_____

Who Could You Pray For Right Now Based On This Scripture?

_____

_____

_____

_____

MAY 19

Then he said to them all: Whoever wants to be my disciple must deny themselves and take up their cross daily and follow me.
Luke 9:23

How Does This Scripture Speak To You?

_____
_____
_____
_____
_____

In What Ways Can You Apply This To Your Life?

_____
_____
_____
_____
_____

Who Could You Pray For Right Now Based On This Scripture?

_____
_____
_____
_____

MAY 20

He answered, "'Love the Lord your God with all your
heart and with all your soul and with all your strength
and with all your mind'; and, 'Love your neighbor as
yourself.'"
Luke 10:27

How Does This Scripture Speak To You?

_____

_____

_____

_____

In What Ways Can You Apply This To Your Life?

_____

_____

_____

_____

Who Could You Pray For Right Now Based On This Scripture?

_____

_____

_____

_____

MAY 21

For those who are led by the Spirit of God are
the children of God.
Romans 8:14

How Does This Scripture Speak To You?

_____
_____
_____
_____
_____

In What Ways Can You Apply This To Your Life?

_____
_____
_____
_____
_____

Who Could You Pray For Right Now Based On This Scripture?

_____
_____
_____
_____

MAY 22

We are witnesses of these things, and so is the
Holy Spirit, whom God has given to those who
obey him.
Acts 5:32

How Does This Scripture Speak To You?

_____
_____
_____
_____
_____

In What Ways Can You Apply This To Your Life?

_____
_____
_____
_____
_____

**Who Could You Pray For Right Now Based On
This Scripture?**

_____
_____
_____
_____

MAY 23

Therefore, I urge you, brothers and sisters, in view of
God's mercy, to offer your bodies as a living sacrifice,
holy and pleasing to God—this is your true and
proper worship.
Romans 12:1

How Does This Scripture Speak To You?

_____

_____

_____

_____

_____

In What Ways Can You Apply This To Your Life?

_____

_____

_____

_____

_____

Who Could You Pray For Right Now Based On This Scripture?

_____

_____

_____

_____

MAY 24

And every tongue acknowledge that Jesus Christ is
Lord, to the glory of God the Father.
Philippians 2:11

How Does This Scripture Speak To You?

_____
_____
_____
_____
_____

In What Ways Can You Apply This To Your Life?

_____
_____
_____
_____
_____

Who Could You Pray For Right Now Based On This Scripture?

_____
_____
_____
_____

MAY 25

So that I may come to you with joy, by God's will, and
in your company be refreshed.
Romans 15:32

How Does This Scripture Speak To You?

_____

_____

_____

_____

_____

In What Ways Can You Apply This To Your Life?

_____

_____

_____

_____

_____

Who Could You Pray For Right Now Based On This Scripture?

_____

_____

_____

_____

MAY 26

Blessed are all who fear the Lord,
who walk in obedience to him.
Psalm 128:1

How Does This Scripture Speak To You?

_____
_____
_____
_____
_____

In What Ways Can You Apply This To Your Life?

_____
_____
_____
_____
_____

Who Could You Pray For Right Now Based On This Scripture?

_____
_____
_____
_____

MAY 27

Whoever believes in the Son has eternal life, but whoever rejects the Son will not see life, for God's wrath remains on them.
John 3:36

How Does This Scripture Speak To You?

_____
_____
_____
_____
_____

In What Ways Can You Apply This To Your Life?

_____
_____
_____
_____
_____

Who Could You Pray For Right Now Based On This Scripture?

_____
_____
_____
_____

MAY 28

For the flesh desires what is contrary to the Spirit,
and the Spirit what is contrary to the flesh. They are in
conflict with each other, so that you are not to do
whatever you want.
Galatians 5:17

How Does This Scripture Speak To You?

_____

_____

_____

_____

_____

In What Ways Can You Apply This To Your Life?

_____

_____

_____

_____

_____

Who Could You Pray For Right Now Based On This Scripture?

_____

_____

_____

_____

MAY 29

The world and its desires pass away, but whoever does the will of God lives forever.
<u>1 John 2:17</u>

How Does This Scripture Speak To You?

_____
_____
_____
_____
_____

In What Ways Can You Apply This To Your Life?

_____
_____
_____
_____
_____

Who Could You Pray For Right Now Based On This Scripture?

_____
_____
_____
_____

MAY 30

Am I now trying to win the approval of human beings, or of God? Or am I trying to please people? If I were still trying to please people, I would not be a servant of Christ.
Galatians 1:10

How Does This Scripture Speak To You?

_____
_____
_____
_____
_____

In What Ways Can You Apply This To Your Life?

_____
_____
_____
_____
_____

Who Could You Pray For Right Now Based On This Scripture?

_____
_____
_____
_____

MAY 31

I will hasten and not delay
to obey your commands.
Psalm 119:60

How Does This Scripture Speak To You?

_____
_____
_____
_____
_____

In What Ways Can You Apply This To Your Life?

_____
_____
_____
_____
_____

Who Could You Pray For Right Now Based On This Scripture?

_____
_____
_____
_____

June

Strength Scriptures

JUNE 1

So do not fear, for I am with you;
do not be dismayed, for I am your God.
I will strengthen you and help you;
I will uphold you with my righteous right hand.
Isaiah 41:10

How Does This Scripture Speak To You?

_____
_____
_____
_____
_____

In What Ways Can You Apply This To Your Life?

_____
_____
_____
_____
_____

Who Could You Pray For Right Now Based On This Scripture?

_____
_____
_____
_____

JUNE 2

But those who hope in the Lord will renew their strength. They will soar on wings like eagles; they will run and not grow weary, they will walk and not be faint.
Isaiah 40:31

How Does This Scripture Speak To You?

_____
_____
_____
_____
_____

In What Ways Can You Apply This To Your Life?

_____
_____
_____
_____
_____

Who Could You Pray For Right Now Based On This Scripture?

_____
_____
_____
_____

JUNE 3

My flesh and my heart may fail,
but God is the strength of my heart
and my portion forever.
Psalm 73:26

How Does This Scripture Speak To You?

_____
_____
_____
_____
_____

In What Ways Can You Apply This To Your Life?

_____
_____
_____
_____
_____

Who Could You Pray For Right Now Based On This Scripture?

_____
_____
_____
_____

JUNE 4

I can do all this through him who gives me strength.
Philippians 4:13

How Does This Scripture Speak To You?

_____
_____
_____
_____
_____

In What Ways Can You Apply This To Your Life?

_____
_____
_____
_____
_____

Who Could You Pray For Right Now Based On This Scripture?

_____
_____
_____
_____

JUNE 5

He gives strength to the weary
and increases the power of the weak.
Isaiah 40:29

How Does This Scripture Speak To You?

_____

_____

_____

_____

_____

In What Ways Can You Apply This To Your Life?

_____

_____

_____

_____

_____

**Who Could You Pray For Right Now Based On
This Scripture?**

_____

_____

_____

_____

JUNE 6

That is why, for Christ's sake, I delight in weaknesses, in
insults, in hardships, in persecutions, in difficulties. For
when I am weak, then I am strong.
2 Corinthians 12:10

How Does This Scripture Speak To You?

_____

_____

_____

_____

_____

In What Ways Can You Apply This To Your Life?

_____

_____

_____

_____

_____

Who Could You Pray For Right Now Based On This Scripture?

_____

_____

_____

_____

JUNE 7

For the Spirit God gave us does not make us timid, but
gives us power, love and self-discipline.
2 Timothy 1:7

How Does This Scripture Speak To You?

_____
_____
_____
_____
_____

In What Ways Can You Apply This To Your Life?

_____
_____
_____
_____
_____

Who Could You Pray For Right Now Based On This Scripture?

_____
_____
_____
_____

JUNE 8

But the Lord is faithful, and he will strengthen you and
protect you from the evil one.
2 Thessalonians 3:3

How Does This Scripture Speak To You?

_____

_____

_____

_____

_____

In What Ways Can You Apply This To Your Life?

_____

_____

_____

_____

_____

Who Could You Pray For Right Now Based On This Scripture?

_____

_____

_____

_____

JUNE 9

I love you, Lord, my strength.
The Lord is my rock, my fortress and my deliverer;
my God is my rock, in whom I take refuge,
my shield and the horn of my salvation, my stronghold.
<u>Psalm 18:1-2</u>

How Does This Scripture Speak To You?

_____

_____

_____

_____

_____

In What Ways Can You Apply This To Your Life?

_____

_____

_____

_____

_____

Who Could You Pray For Right Now Based On This Scripture?

_____

_____

_____

_____

JUNE 10

Look to the Lord and his strength;
seek his face always.
<u>1 Chronicles 16:11</u>

How Does This Scripture Speak To You?

_____
_____
_____
_____
_____

In What Ways Can You Apply This To Your Life?

_____
_____
_____
_____
_____

Who Could You Pray For Right Now Based On This Scripture?

_____
_____
_____
_____

JUNE 11

Be on your guard; stand firm in the faith;
be courageous; be strong.
1 Corinthians 16:13

How Does This Scripture Speak To You?

_____
_____
_____
_____
_____

In What Ways Can You Apply This To Your Life?

_____
_____
_____
_____
_____

Who Could You Pray For Right Now Based On This Scripture?

_____
_____
_____
_____

JUNE 12

But I will sing of your strength,
in the morning I will sing of your love;
for you are my fortress,
my refuge in times of trouble.
Psalm 59:16

How Does This Scripture Speak To You?

_____
_____
_____
_____
_____

In What Ways Can You Apply This To Your Life?

_____
_____
_____
_____
_____

Who Could You Pray For Right Now Based On This Scripture?

_____
_____
_____
_____

JUNE 13

Ah, Sovereign Lord, you have made the heavens and
the earth by your great power and outstretched arm.
Nothing is too hard for you.
Jeremiah 32:17

How Does This Scripture Speak To You?

_____

_____

_____

_____

_____

In What Ways Can You Apply This To Your Life?

_____

_____

_____

_____

_____

**Who Could You Pray For Right Now Based On
This Scripture?**

_____

_____

_____

_____

JUNE 14

The Sovereign Lord is my strength;
he makes my feet like the feet of a deer,
he enables me to tread on the heights.
Habakkuk 3:19

How Does This Scripture Speak To You?

_____
_____
_____
_____
_____

In What Ways Can You Apply This To Your Life?

_____
_____
_____
_____
_____

Who Could You Pray For Right Now Based On This Scripture?

_____
_____
_____
_____

JUNE 15

Finally, be strong in the Lord and in his mighty power.
Ephesians 6:10

How Does This Scripture Speak To You?

_____

_____

_____

_____

_____

In What Ways Can You Apply This To Your Life?

_____

_____

_____

_____

_____

Who Could You Pray For Right Now Based On This Scripture?

_____

_____

_____

_____

JUNE 16

For the word of God is alive and active. Sharper than any double-edged sword, it penetrates even to dividing soul and spirit, joints and marrow; it judges the thoughts and attitudes of the heart.
Hebrews 4:12

How Does This Scripture Speak To You?

_____
_____
_____
_____
_____

In What Ways Can You Apply This To Your Life?

_____
_____
_____
_____
_____

Who Could You Pray For Right Now Based On This Scripture?

_____
_____
_____

JUNE 17

Yours, Lord, is the greatness and the power
and the glory and the majesty and the splendor,
for everything in heaven and earth is yours. Yours,
Lord, is the kingdom; you are exalted as head over all.
1 Chronicles 29:11

How Does This Scripture Speak To You?

_____
_____
_____
_____
_____

In What Ways Can You Apply This To Your Life?

_____
_____
_____
_____
_____

Who Could You Pray For Right Now Based On This Scripture?

_____
_____
_____
_____

JUNE 18

The Lord is my strength and my shield;
my heart trusts in him, and he helps me.
My heart leaps for joy,
and with my song I praise him.
Psalm 28:7

How Does This Scripture Speak To You?

_____
_____
_____
_____
_____

In What Ways Can You Apply This To Your Life?

_____
_____
_____
_____
_____

Who Could You Pray For Right Now Based On This Scripture?

_____
_____
_____
_____

JUNE 19

Now to him who is able to do immeasurably more than all we ask or imagine, according to his power that is at work within us, to him be glory in the church and in Christ Jesus throughout all generations, for ever and ever! Amen. Ephesians 3:20-21

How Does This Scripture Speak To You?

_____
_____
_____
_____
_____

In What Ways Can You Apply This To Your Life?

_____
_____
_____
_____
_____

Who Could You Pray For Right Now Based On This Scripture?

_____
_____
_____
_____

JUNE 20

Love the Lord your God with all your heart and with all
your soul and with all your mind and with all your
strength.
Mark 12:30

How Does This Scripture Speak To You?

_____

_____

_____

_____

_____

In What Ways Can You Apply This To Your Life?

_____

_____

_____

_____

_____

Who Could You Pray For Right Now Based On This Scripture?

_____

_____

_____

_____

JUNE 21

So he said to me, "This is the word of the Lord to
Zerubbabel: 'Not by might nor by power, but by my
Spirit,' says the Lord Almighty."
Zechariah 4:6

How Does This Scripture Speak To You?

_____
_____
_____
_____
_____

In What Ways Can You Apply This To Your Life?

_____
_____
_____
_____
_____

Who Could You Pray For Right Now Based On This Scripture?

_____
_____
_____
_____

JUNE 22

For the message of the cross is foolishness to those who are perishing, but to us who are being saved it is the power of God.
1 Corinthians 1:18

How Does This Scripture Speak To You?

_____
_____
_____
_____
_____

In What Ways Can You Apply This To Your Life?

_____
_____
_____
_____
_____

Who Could You Pray For Right Now Based On This Scripture?

_____
_____
_____

JUNE 23

For who is God besides the Lord?
And who is the Rock except our God?
Psalm 18:31

How Does This Scripture Speak To You?

_____
_____
_____
_____
_____

In What Ways Can You Apply This To Your Life?

_____
_____
_____
_____
_____

Who Could You Pray For Right Now Based On This Scripture?

_____
_____
_____
_____

JUNE 24

For since the creation of the world God's invisible qualities—his eternal power and divine nature—have been clearly seen, being understood from what has been made, so that people are without excuse.
Romans 1:20

How Does This Scripture Speak To You?

_____

_____

_____

_____

In What Ways Can You Apply This To Your Life?

_____

_____

_____

_____

Who Could You Pray For Right Now Based On This Scripture?

_____

_____

_____

JUNE 25

It was not by their sword that they won the land,
nor did their arm bring them victory;
it was your right hand, your arm,
and the light of your face, for you loved them.
Psalm 44:3

How Does This Scripture Speak To You?

_____
_____
_____
_____
_____

In What Ways Can You Apply This To Your Life?

_____
_____
_____
_____
_____

Who Could You Pray For Right Now Based On This Scripture?

_____
_____
_____
_____

JUNE 26

For in Christ all the fullness of the Deity lives in bodily form, and in Christ you have been brought to fullness. He is the head over every power and authority.
Colossians 2:9-10

How Does This Scripture Speak To You?

_____

_____

_____

_____

_____

In What Ways Can You Apply This To Your Life?

_____

_____

_____

_____

_____

Who Could You Pray For Right Now Based On This Scripture?

_____

_____

_____

_____

JUNE 27

Though one may be overpowered,
two can defend themselves.
A cord of three strands is not quickly broken.
Ecclesiastes 4:12

How Does This Scripture Speak To You?

_____
_____
_____
_____
_____

In What Ways Can You Apply This To Your Life?

_____
_____
_____
_____
_____

Who Could You Pray For Right Now Based On This Scripture?

_____
_____
_____
_____

JUNE 28

The Lord gives strength to his people;
the Lord blesses his people with peace.
Psalm 29:11

How Does This Scripture Speak To You?

_____
_____
_____
_____
_____

In What Ways Can You Apply This To Your Life?

_____
_____
_____
_____
_____

Who Could You Pray For Right Now Based On This Scripture?

_____
_____
_____
_____

JUNE 29

Wealth and honor come from you;
you are the ruler of all things.
In your hands are strength and power
to exalt and give strength to all.
1 Chronicles 29:12

How Does This Scripture Speak To You?

_____

_____

_____

_____

_____

In What Ways Can You Apply This To Your Life?

_____

_____

_____

_____

_____

Who Could You Pray For Right Now Based On This Scripture?

_____

_____

_____

_____

JUNE 30

The Almighty is beyond our reach and exalted in
power; in his justice and great righteousness,
he does not oppress.
Job 37:23

How Does This Scripture Speak To You?

_____

_____

_____

_____

_____

In What Ways Can You Apply This To Your Life?

_____

_____

_____

_____

_____

Who Could You Pray For Right Now Based On
This Scripture?

_____

_____

_____

_____

July

Grace Scriptures

JULY 1

Let us then approach God's throne of grace with confidence, so that we may receive mercy and find grace to help us in our time of need.
Hebrews 4:16

How Does This Scripture Speak To You?

_____

_____

_____

_____

_____

In What Ways Can You Apply This To Your Life?

_____

_____

_____

_____

_____

Who Could You Pray For Right Now Based On This Scripture?

_____

_____

_____

_____

JULY 2

"The Lord bless you and keep you;
the Lord make his face shine on you and be gracious to
you; the Lord turn his face toward you
and give you peace."
Numbers 6:24-26

How Does This Scripture Speak To You?

_____
_____
_____
_____
_____

In What Ways Can You Apply This To Your Life?

_____
_____
_____
_____
_____

Who Could You Pray For Right Now Based On This Scripture?

_____
_____
_____
_____

JULY 3

But because of his great love for us, God, who is rich in mercy, made us alive with Christ even when we were dead in transgressions—it is by grace you have been saved.
Ephesians 2:4-5

How Does This Scripture Speak To You?

_____

_____

_____

_____

_____

In What Ways Can You Apply This To Your Life?

_____

_____

_____

_____

_____

Who Could You Pray For Right Now Based On This Scripture?

_____

_____

_____

_____

JULY 4

The Lord is compassionate and gracious,
slow to anger, abounding in love.
Psalm 103:8

How Does This Scripture Speak To You?

_____
_____
_____
_____
_____

In What Ways Can You Apply This To Your Life?

_____
_____
_____
_____
_____

Who Could You Pray For Right Now Based On This Scripture?

_____
_____
_____
_____

JULY 5

And the God of all grace, who called you to his eternal glory in Christ, after you have suffered a little while, will himself restore you and make you strong, firm and steadfast.
1 Peter 5:10

How Does This Scripture Speak To You?

_____
_____
_____
_____
_____

In What Ways Can You Apply This To Your Life?

_____
_____
_____
_____
_____

Who Could You Pray For Right Now Based On This Scripture?

_____
_____
_____
_____

JULY 6

For if you forgive other people when they sin
against you, your heavenly Father will also forgive you.
Matthew 6:14

How Does This Scripture Speak To You?

_____

_____

_____

_____

_____

In What Ways Can You Apply This To Your Life?

_____

_____

_____

_____

_____

Who Could You Pray For Right Now Based On This Scripture?

_____

_____

_____

_____

JULY 7

For the grace of God has appeared that offers salvation
to all people. It teaches us to say "No" to ungodliness
and worldly passions, and to live self-controlled, upright
and godly lives in this present age.
Titus 2:11-12

How Does This Scripture Speak To You?

_____
_____
_____
_____
_____

In What Ways Can You Apply This To Your Life?

_____
_____
_____
_____

Who Could You Pray For Right Now Based On This Scripture?

_____
_____
_____
_____

JULY 8

Yet the Lord longs to be gracious to you;
therefore he will rise up to show you compassion.
For the Lord is a God of justice.
Blessed are all who wait for him!
<u>Isaiah 30:18</u>

How Does This Scripture Speak To You?

_____

_____

_____

_____

_____

In What Ways Can You Apply This To Your Life?

_____

_____

_____

_____

_____

Who Could You Pray For Right Now Based On This Scripture?

_____

_____

_____

_____

JULY 9

He has saved us and called us to a holy life—not because of anything we have done but because of his own purpose and grace. This grace was given us in Christ Jesus before the beginning of time.
2 Timothy 1:9

How Does This Scripture Speak To You?

_____

_____

_____

_____

_____

In What Ways Can You Apply This To Your Life?

_____

_____

_____

_____

_____

Who Could You Pray For Right Now Based On This Scripture?

_____

_____

_____

_____

JULY 10

For sin shall no longer be your master, because you are
not under the law, but under grace.
Romans 6:14

How Does This Scripture Speak To You?

_____
_____
_____
_____
_____

In What Ways Can You Apply This To Your Life?

_____
_____
_____
_____
_____

Who Could You Pray For Right Now Based On This Scripture?

_____
_____
_____
_____

JULY 11

The grace of the Lord Jesus be with God's people.
Amen.
Revelation 22:21

How Does This Scripture Speak To You?

_____
_____
_____
_____
_____

In What Ways Can You Apply This To Your Life?

_____
_____
_____
_____
_____

Who Could You Pray For Right Now Based On This Scripture?

_____
_____
_____
_____

JULY 12

What then? Shall we sin because we are not under the
law but under grace? By no means!
Romans 6:15

How Does This Scripture Speak To You?

_____

_____

_____

_____

_____

In What Ways Can You Apply This To Your Life?

_____

_____

_____

_____

_____

Who Could You Pray For Right Now Based On This Scripture?

_____

_____

_____

_____

JULY 13

For all have sinned and fall short of the glory of God, and all are justified freely by his grace through the redemption that came by Christ Jesus.
Romans 3:23-24

How Does This Scripture Speak To You?

_____
_____
_____
_____
_____

In What Ways Can You Apply This To Your Life?

_____
_____
_____
_____
_____

Who Could You Pray For Right Now Based On This Scripture?

_____
_____
_____
_____

JULY 14

May the favor of the Lord our God rest on us;
establish the work of our hands for us—
yes, establish the work of our hands.
Psalm 90:17

How Does This Scripture Speak To You?

_____
_____
_____
_____
_____

In What Ways Can You Apply This To Your Life?

_____
_____
_____
_____

Who Could You Pray For Right Now Based On This Scripture?

_____
_____
_____

JULY 15

For God so loved the world that he gave his one and only Son, that whoever believes in him shall not perish but have eternal life.
John 3:16

How Does This Scripture Speak To You?

_____

_____

_____

_____

_____

In What Ways Can You Apply This To Your Life?

_____

_____

_____

_____

_____

Who Could You Pray For Right Now Based On This Scripture?

_____

_____

_____

_____

JULY 16

The grace of the Lord Jesus Christ be with your spirit.
Philemon 1:25

How Does This Scripture Speak To You?

_____

_____

_____

_____

_____

In What Ways Can You Apply This To Your Life?

_____

_____

_____

_____

_____

Who Could You Pray For Right Now Based On This Scripture?

_____

_____

_____

_____

JULY 17

Therefore, with minds that are alert and fully sober, set
your hope on the grace to be brought to you when
Jesus Christ is revealed at his coming.
1 Peter 1:13

How Does This Scripture Speak To You?

_____

_____

_____

_____

_____

In What Ways Can You Apply This To Your Life?

_____

_____

_____

_____

_____

**Who Could You Pray For Right Now Based On
This Scripture?**

_____

_____

_____

_____

JULY 18

But the gift is not like the trespass. For if the many
died by the trespass of the one man, how much more
did God's grace and the gift that came by the grace of
the one man, Jesus Christ, overflow to the many!
Romans 5:15

How Does This Scripture Speak To You?

_____

_____

_____

_____

_____

In What Ways Can You Apply This To Your Life?

_____

_____

_____

_____

_____

Who Could You Pray For Right Now Based On This Scripture?

_____

_____

_____

_____

JULY 19

So that, just as sin reigned in death, so also grace
might reign through righteousness to bring eternal
life through Jesus Christ our Lord.
Romans 5:21

How Does This Scripture Speak To You?

_____
_____
_____
_____
_____

In What Ways Can You Apply This To Your Life?

_____
_____
_____
_____
_____

Who Could You Pray For Right Now Based On This Scripture?

_____
_____
_____
_____

JULY 20

Surely your goodness and love will follow me
all the days of my life,
and I will dwell in the house of the Lord
forever.
Psalm 23:6

How Does This Scripture Speak To You?

_____

_____

_____

_____

_____

In What Ways Can You Apply This To Your Life?

_____

_____

_____

_____

_____

Who Could You Pray For Right Now Based On This Scripture?

_____

_____

_____

_____

JULY 21

For the Lord your God is gracious and compassionate.
He will not turn his face from you if you return to him.
2 Chronicles 30:9b

How Does This Scripture Speak To You?

_____
_____
_____
_____
_____

In What Ways Can You Apply This To Your Life?

_____
_____
_____
_____
_____

Who Could You Pray For Right Now Based On This Scripture?

_____
_____
_____
_____

JULY 22

For it is by grace you have been saved, through faith—
and this is not from yourselves, it is the gift of God—
not by works, so that no one can boast.
Ephesians 2:8-9

How Does This Scripture Speak To You?

_____

_____

_____

_____

_____

In What Ways Can You Apply This To Your Life?

_____

_____

_____

_____

_____

Who Could You Pray For Right Now Based On This Scripture?

_____

_____

_____

_____

JULY 23

Whoever conceals their sins does not prosper,
but the one who confesses and renounces them finds
mercy.
Proverbs 28:13

How Does This Scripture Speak To You?

_____
_____
_____
_____
_____

In What Ways Can You Apply This To Your Life?

_____
_____
_____
_____
_____

Who Could You Pray For Right Now Based On This Scripture?

_____
_____
_____
_____

JULY 24

Out of the depths I cry to you, Lord;
Lord, hear my voice.
Let your ears be attentive
to my cry for mercy.
Psalm 130:1-2

How Does This Scripture Speak To You?

_____
_____
_____
_____
_____

In What Ways Can You Apply This To Your Life?

_____
_____
_____
_____

Who Could You Pray For Right Now Based On This Scripture?

_____
_____
_____

JULY 25

However, I consider my life worth nothing to me; my only aim is to finish the race and complete the task the Lord Jesus has given me—the task of testifying to the good news of God's grace.

<u>Acts 20:24</u>

How Does This Scripture Speak To You?

_____
_____
_____
_____
_____

In What Ways Can You Apply This To Your Life?

_____
_____
_____
_____
_____

Who Could You Pray For Right Now Based On This Scripture?

_____
_____
_____
_____

JULY 26

But grow in the grace and knowledge of our Lord and
Savior Jesus Christ. To him be glory both now and
forever! Amen.
2 Peter 3:18

How Does This Scripture Speak To You?

_____
_____
_____
_____
_____

In What Ways Can You Apply This To Your Life?

_____
_____
_____
_____
_____

Who Could You Pray For Right Now Based On This Scripture?

_____
_____
_____
_____

JULY 27

The grace of the Lord Jesus Christ be with your spirit. Amen.
Philippians 4:23

How Does This Scripture Speak To You?

_____

_____

_____

_____

_____

In What Ways Can You Apply This To Your Life?

_____

_____

_____

_____

_____

Who Could You Pray For Right Now Based On This Scripture?

_____

_____

_____

_____

JULY 28

What shall we say, then? Shall we go on sinning so that grace may increase? By no means! We are those who have died to sin; how can we live in it any longer?
Romans 6:1-2

How Does This Scripture Speak To You?

_____

_____

_____

_____

_____

In What Ways Can You Apply This To Your Life?

_____

_____

_____

_____

_____

Who Could You Pray For Right Now Based On This Scripture?

_____

_____

_____

_____

JULY 29

For by the grace given me I say to every one of you:
Do not think of yourself more highly than you ought,
but rather think of yourself with sober judgment, in
accordance with the faith God has distributed to
each of you. Romans 12:3

How Does This Scripture Speak To You?

_____

_____

_____

_____

_____

In What Ways Can You Apply This To Your Life?

_____

_____

_____

_____

_____

**Who Could You Pray For Right Now Based On
This Scripture?**

_____

_____

_____

_____

JULY 30

For it has been granted to you on behalf of Christ not
only to believe in him, but also to suffer for him.
Philippians 1:29

How Does This Scripture Speak To You?

_____

_____

_____

_____

_____

In What Ways Can You Apply This To Your Life?

_____

_____

_____

_____

_____

Who Could You Pray For Right Now Based On This Scripture?

_____

_____

_____

_____

JULY 31

But he said to me, "My grace is sufficient for you, for my power is made perfect in weakness." Therefore I will boast all the more gladly about my weaknesses, so that Christ's power may rest on me.
2 Corinthians 12:9

How Does This Scripture Speak To You?

_____
_____
_____
_____
_____

In What Ways Can You Apply This To Your Life?

_____
_____
_____
_____
_____

Who Could You Pray For Right Now Based On This Scripture?

_____
_____
_____
_____

August

Heart Scriptures

AUGUST 1

Above all else, guard your heart,
for everything you do flows from it.
Proverbs 4:23

How Does This Scripture Speak To You?

_____
_____
_____
_____
_____

In What Ways Can You Apply This To Your Life?

_____
_____
_____
_____
_____

Who Could You Pray For Right Now Based On This Scripture?

_____
_____
_____
_____

AUGUST 2

As water reflects the face,
so one's life reflects the heart.
Proverbs 27:19

How Does This Scripture Speak To You?

_____
_____
_____
_____
_____

In What Ways Can You Apply This To Your Life?

_____
_____
_____
_____
_____

Who Could You Pray For Right Now Based On This Scripture?

_____
_____
_____
_____

AUGUST 3

The heart is deceitful above all things and beyond cure. Who can understand it? "I the Lord search the heart and examine the mind, to reward each person according to their conduct, according to what their deeds deserve." Jeremiah 17:9-10

How Does This Scripture Speak To You?

_____

_____

_____

_____

_____

In What Ways Can You Apply This To Your Life?

_____

_____

_____

_____

_____

Who Could You Pray For Right Now Based On This Scripture?

_____

_____

_____

_____

AUGUST 4

Your beauty should not come from outward
adornment, such as elaborate hairstyles and the wearing
of gold jewelry or fine clothes. Rather, it should be that
of your inner self, the unfading beauty of a gentle and quiet
spirit, which is of great worth in God's sight.
1 Peter 3:3-4

How Does This Scripture Speak To You?

_____

_____

_____

_____

_____

In What Ways Can You Apply This To Your Life?

_____

_____

_____

_____

_____

Who Could You Pray For Right Now Based On This Scripture?

_____

_____

_____

_____

AUGUST 5

May he give you the desire of your heart
and make all your plans succeed.
Psalm 20:4

How Does This Scripture Speak To You?

_____
_____
_____
_____
_____

In What Ways Can You Apply This To Your Life?

_____
_____
_____
_____
_____

Who Could You Pray For Right Now Based On This Scripture?

_____
_____
_____
_____

AUGUST 6

You will seek me and find me when you seek me with all your heart.
Jeremiah 29:13

How Does This Scripture Speak To You?

_____
_____
_____
_____
_____

In What Ways Can You Apply This To Your Life?

_____
_____
_____
_____
_____

Who Could You Pray For Right Now Based On This Scripture?

_____
_____
_____
_____

AUGUST 7

Let love and faithfulness never leave you; bind them around your neck, write them on the tablet of your heart. Then you will win favor and a good name in the sight of God and man.
Proverbs 3:3-4

How Does This Scripture Speak To You?

_____
_____
_____
_____
_____

In What Ways Can You Apply This To Your Life?

_____
_____
_____
_____
_____

Who Could You Pray For Right Now Based On This Scripture?

_____
_____
_____
_____

AUGUST 8

Create in me a pure heart, O God,
and renew a steadfast spirit within me.
Psalm 51:10

How Does This Scripture Speak To You?

_____
_____
_____
_____
_____

In What Ways Can You Apply This To Your Life?

_____
_____
_____
_____
_____

Who Could You Pray For Right Now Based On This Scripture?

_____
_____
_____
_____

AUGUST 9

Trust in the Lord with all your heart
and lean not on your own understanding;
in all your ways submit to him,
and he will make your paths straight.
Proverbs 3:5-6

How Does This Scripture Speak To You?

_____
_____
_____
_____
_____

In What Ways Can You Apply This To Your Life?

_____
_____
_____
_____
_____

Who Could You Pray For Right Now Based On This Scripture?

_____
_____
_____
_____

AUGUST 10

But the Lord said to Samuel, "Do not consider his appearance or his height, for I have rejected him. The Lord does not look at the things people look at. People look at the outward appearance, but the Lord looks at the heart." 1 Samuel 16:7

How Does This Scripture Speak To You?

_____

_____

_____

_____

_____

In What Ways Can You Apply This To Your Life?

_____

_____

_____

_____

_____

Who Could You Pray For Right Now Based On This Scripture?

_____

_____

_____

_____

AUGUST 11

Jesus replied: 'Love the Lord your God with all your heart and with all your soul and with all your mind.'
Matthew 22:37

How Does This Scripture Speak To You?

_____

_____

_____

_____

_____

In What Ways Can You Apply This To Your Life?

_____

_____

_____

_____

Who Could You Pray For Right Now Based On This Scripture?

_____

_____

_____

_____

AUGUST 12

Take delight in the Lord,
and he will give you the desires of your heart.
Psalm 37:4

How Does This Scripture Speak To You?

_____
_____
_____
_____
_____

In What Ways Can You Apply This To Your Life?

_____
_____
_____
_____
_____

Who Could You Pray For Right Now Based On This Scripture?

_____
_____
_____
_____

AUGUST 13

Each of you should give what you have decided in your heart to give, not reluctantly or under compulsion, for God loves a cheerful giver.
2 Corinthians 9:7

How Does This Scripture Speak To You?

_____
_____
_____
_____
_____

In What Ways Can You Apply This To Your Life?

_____
_____
_____
_____
_____

Who Could You Pray For Right Now Based On This Scripture?

_____
_____
_____
_____

AUGUST 14

A cheerful heart is good medicine,
but a crushed spirit dries up the bones.
Proverbs 17:22

How Does This Scripture Speak To You?

_____
_____
_____
_____
_____

In What Ways Can You Apply This To Your Life?

_____
_____
_____
_____
_____

Who Could You Pray For Right Now Based On This Scripture?

_____
_____
_____
_____

AUGUST 15

My son, do not forget my teaching,
but keep my commands in your heart,
for they will prolong your life many years
and bring you peace and prosperity.
Proverbs 3:1-2

How Does This Scripture Speak To You?

_____

_____

_____

_____

_____

In What Ways Can You Apply This To Your Life?

_____

_____

_____

_____

_____

Who Could You Pray For Right Now Based On This Scripture?

_____

_____

_____

_____

AUGUST 16

For where your treasure is, there your heart will be also.
Matthew 6:21

How Does This Scripture Speak To You?

_____
_____
_____
_____
_____

In What Ways Can You Apply This To Your Life?

_____
_____
_____
_____
_____

Who Could You Pray For Right Now Based On This Scripture?

_____
_____
_____
_____

AUGUST 17

The wise in heart accept commands,
but a chattering fool comes to ruin.
Proverbs 10:8

How Does This Scripture Speak To You?

_____
_____
_____
_____
_____

In What Ways Can You Apply This To Your Life?

_____
_____
_____
_____
_____

Who Could You Pray For Right Now Based On This Scripture?

_____
_____
_____
_____

AUGUST 18

Be strong and take heart,
all you who hope in the Lord.
Psalm 31:24

How Does This Scripture Speak To You?

_____
_____
_____
_____
_____

In What Ways Can You Apply This To Your Life?

_____
_____
_____
_____
_____

Who Could You Pray For Right Now Based On This Scripture?

_____
_____
_____
_____

AUGUST 19

I seek you with all my heart;
do not let me stray from your commands.
Psalm 119:10

How Does This Scripture Speak To You?

_____
_____
_____
_____
_____

In What Ways Can You Apply This To Your Life?

_____
_____
_____
_____
_____

Who Could You Pray For Right Now Based On This Scripture?

_____
_____
_____
_____

AUGUST 20

Teach us to number our days,
that we may gain a heart of wisdom.
Psalm 90:12

How Does This Scripture Speak To You?

_____
_____
_____
_____
_____

In What Ways Can You Apply This To Your Life?

_____
_____
_____
_____
_____

Who Could You Pray For Right Now Based On This Scripture?

_____
_____
_____
_____

AUGUST 21

May these words of my mouth and this meditation
of my heart be pleasing in your sight,
Lord, my Rock and my Redeemer.
Psalm 19:14

How Does This Scripture Speak To You?

_____

_____

_____

_____

_____

In What Ways Can You Apply This To Your Life?

_____

_____

_____

_____

_____

Who Could You Pray For Right Now Based On This Scripture?

_____

_____

_____

_____

AUGUST 22

Blessed are those who keep his statutes
and seek him with all their heart.
Psalm 119:2

How Does This Scripture Speak To You?

_____
_____
_____
_____
_____

In What Ways Can You Apply This To Your Life?

_____
_____
_____
_____
_____

Who Could You Pray For Right Now Based On This Scripture?

_____
_____
_____
_____

AUGUST 23

But be very careful to keep the commandment and the law that Moses the servant of the Lord gave you: to love the Lord your God, to walk in obedience to him, to keep his commands, to hold fast to him and to serve him with all your heart and with all your soul.
Joshua 22:5

How Does This Scripture Speak To You?

_____

_____

_____

_____

_____

In What Ways Can You Apply This To Your Life?

_____

_____

_____

_____

_____

Who Could You Pray For Right Now Based On This Scripture?

_____

_____

_____

_____

AUGUST 24

Truly I tell you, if anyone says to this mountain, 'Go, throw yourself into the sea,' and does not doubt in their heart but believes that what they say will happen, it will be done for them.

Mark 11:23

How Does This Scripture Speak To You?

_____

_____

_____

_____

_____

In What Ways Can You Apply This To Your Life?

_____

_____

_____

_____

_____

Who Could You Pray For Right Now Based On This Scripture?

_____

_____

_____

_____

AUGUST 25

I will praise you with an upright heart
as I learn your righteous laws.
Psalm 119:7

How Does This Scripture Speak To You?

_____
_____
_____
_____
_____

In What Ways Can You Apply This To Your Life?

_____
_____
_____
_____
_____

Who Could You Pray For Right Now Based On This Scripture?

_____
_____
_____
_____

AUGUST 26

Your statutes are my heritage forever;
they are the joy of my heart.
Psalm 119:111

How Does This Scripture Speak To You?

_____
_____
_____
_____
_____

In What Ways Can You Apply This To Your Life?

_____
_____
_____
_____
_____

Who Could You Pray For Right Now Based On This Scripture?

_____
_____
_____
_____

AUGUST 27

Hope deferred makes the heart sick,
but a longing fulfilled is a tree of life.
Proverbs 13:12

How Does This Scripture Speak To You?

_____

_____

_____

_____

_____

In What Ways Can You Apply This To Your Life?

_____

_____

_____

_____

_____

Who Could You Pray For Right Now Based On This Scripture?

_____

_____

_____

_____

AUGUST 28

He heals the brokenhearted
and binds up their wounds.
Psalm 147:3

How Does This Scripture Speak To You?

_____

_____

_____

_____

_____

In What Ways Can You Apply This To Your Life?

_____

_____

_____

_____

_____

Who Could You Pray For Right Now Based On This Scripture?

_____

_____

_____

_____

AUGUST 29

Blessed are the pure in heart,
for they will see God.
Matthew 5:8

How Does This Scripture Speak To You?

_____
_____
_____
_____
_____

In What Ways Can You Apply This To Your Life?

_____
_____
_____
_____
_____

Who Could You Pray For Right Now Based On This Scripture?

_____
_____
_____
_____

AUGUST 30

I will give you a new heart and put a new spirit in you;
I will remove from you your heart of stone and give
you a heart of flesh.
Ezekiel 36:26

How Does This Scripture Speak To You?

_____

_____

_____

_____

_____

In What Ways Can You Apply This To Your Life?

_____

_____

_____

_____

_____

Who Could You Pray For Right Now Based On This Scripture?

_____

_____

_____

_____

AUGUST 31

Go, eat your food with gladness, and drink your wine
with a joyful heart, for God has already approved
what you do.
Ecclesiastes 9:7

How Does This Scripture Speak To You?

_____

_____

_____

_____

_____

In What Ways Can You Apply This To Your Life?

_____

_____

_____

_____

_____

Who Could You Pray For Right Now Based On This Scripture?

_____

_____

_____

_____

September

Worship Scriptures

SEPTEMBER 1

Lord, you are my God; I will exalt you and praise your
name, for in perfect faithfulness you have done
wonderful things, things planned long ago.
Isaiah 25:1

How Does This Scripture Speak To You?

_____

_____

_____

_____

_____

In What Ways Can You Apply This To Your Life?

_____

_____

_____

_____

_____

Who Could You Pray For Right Now Based On This Scripture?

_____

_____

_____

_____

SEPTEMBER 2

Worship the Lord your God, and his blessing will be
on your food and water. I will take away sickness
from among you.
Exodus 23:25

How Does This Scripture Speak To You?

_____
_____
_____
_____
_____

In What Ways Can You Apply This To Your Life?

_____
_____
_____
_____
_____

Who Could You Pray For Right Now Based On This Scripture?

_____
_____
_____

SEPTEMBER 3

Let everything that has breath praise the Lord.
Praise the Lord.
Psalm 150:6

How Does This Scripture Speak To You?

_____
_____
_____
_____
_____

In What Ways Can You Apply This To Your Life?

_____
_____
_____
_____
_____

Who Could You Pray For Right Now Based On This Scripture?

_____
_____
_____
_____

SEPTEMBER 4

About midnight Paul and Silas were praying and
singing hymns to God, and the other prisoners were
listening to them.
Acts 16:25

How Does This Scripture Speak To You?

_____

_____

_____

_____

_____

In What Ways Can You Apply This To Your Life?

_____

_____

_____

_____

_____

Who Could You Pray For Right Now Based On This Scripture?

_____

_____

_____

_____

SEPTEMBER 5

God is spirit, and his worshipers must worship in the
Spirit and in truth.
John 4:24

How Does This Scripture Speak To You?

_____

_____

_____

_____

_____

In What Ways Can You Apply This To Your Life?

_____

_____

_____

_____

_____

Who Could You Pray For Right Now Based On This Scripture?

_____

_____

_____

_____

SEPTEMBER 6

Praise the Lord, my soul;
all my inmost being, praise his holy name.
Psalm 103:1

How Does This Scripture Speak To You?

_____
_____
_____
_____
_____

In What Ways Can You Apply This To Your Life?

_____
_____
_____
_____
_____

Who Could You Pray For Right Now Based On This Scripture?

_____
_____
_____
_____

SEPTEMBER 7

Give thanks to the Lord, for he is good;
his love endures forever.
1 Chronicles 16:34

How Does This Scripture Speak To You?

_____
_____
_____
_____
_____

In What Ways Can You Apply This To Your Life?

_____
_____
_____
_____
_____

Who Could You Pray For Right Now Based On This Scripture?

_____
_____
_____
_____

SEPTEMBER 8

You, God, are my God, earnestly I seek you;
I thirst for you, my whole being longs for you,
in a dry and parched land where there is no water.
Psalm 63:1

How Does This Scripture Speak To You?

_____
_____
_____
_____
_____

In What Ways Can You Apply This To Your Life?

_____
_____
_____
_____
_____

Who Could You Pray For Right Now Based On This Scripture?

_____
_____
_____
_____

SEPTEMBER 9

Though the fig tree does not bud and there are no
grapes on the vines, though the olive crop fails
and the fields produce no food, though there are no
sheep in the pen and no cattle in the stalls, yet I will
rejoice in the Lord, I will be joyful in God my Savior.
Habakkuk 3:17-18

How Does This Scripture Speak To You?

_____

_____

_____

_____

_____

In What Ways Can You Apply This To Your Life?

_____

_____

_____

_____

_____

Who Could You Pray For Right Now Based On This Scripture?

_____

_____

_____

_____

SEPTEMBER 10

My mouth is filled with your praise,
declaring your splendor all day long.
Psalm 71:8

How Does This Scripture Speak To You?

_____
_____
_____
_____
_____

In What Ways Can You Apply This To Your Life?

_____
_____
_____
_____
_____

Who Could You Pray For Right Now Based On This Scripture?

_____
_____
_____
_____

SEPTEMBER 11

Yours, Lord, is the greatness and the power and the glory and the majesty and the splendor, for everything in heaven and earth is yours. Yours, Lord, is the kingdom; you are exalted as head over all.
1 Chronicles 29:11

How Does This Scripture Speak To You?

_____
_____
_____
_____
_____

In What Ways Can You Apply This To Your Life?

_____
_____
_____
_____
_____

Who Could You Pray For Right Now Based On This Scripture?

_____
_____
_____
_____

SEPTEMBER 12

Praise be to the God and Father of our Lord Jesus Christ, the Father of compassion and the God of all comfort, who comforts us in all our troubles, so that we can comfort those in any trouble with the comfort we ourselves receive from God.
2 Corinthians 1:3-4

How Does This Scripture Speak To You?

_____

_____

_____

_____

_____

In What Ways Can You Apply This To Your Life?

_____

_____

_____

_____

_____

Who Could You Pray For Right Now Based On This Scripture?

_____

_____

_____

_____

SEPTEMBER 13

How great you are, Sovereign Lord! There is no one like you, and there is no God but you, as we have heard with our own ears.
2 Samuel 7:22

How Does This Scripture Speak To You?

_____
_____
_____
_____
_____

In What Ways Can You Apply This To Your Life?

_____
_____
_____
_____
_____

Who Could You Pray For Right Now Based On This Scripture?

_____
_____
_____
_____

SEPTEMBER 14

Sing to God, sing in praise of his name, extol him who
rides on the clouds; rejoice before him — his name
is the Lord. A father to the fatherless, a defender of
widows, is God in his holy dwelling.
Psalm 68:4-5

How Does This Scripture Speak To You?

_____

_____

_____

_____

In What Ways Can You Apply This To Your Life?

_____

_____

_____

_____

Who Could You Pray For Right Now Based On This Scripture?

_____

_____

_____

SEPTEMBER 15

For from him and through him and for him are all
things. To him be the glory forever! Amen.
Romans 11:36

How Does This Scripture Speak To You?

_____
_____
_____
_____
_____

In What Ways Can You Apply This To Your Life?

_____
_____
_____
_____
_____

Who Could You Pray For Right Now Based On This Scripture?

_____
_____
_____
_____

SEPTEMBER 16

Then you will call on me and come and pray to me,
and I will listen to you.
Jeremiah 29:12

How Does This Scripture Speak To You?

_____
_____
_____
_____
_____

In What Ways Can You Apply This To Your Life?

_____
_____
_____
_____
_____

Who Could You Pray For Right Now Based On This Scripture?

_____
_____
_____
_____

SEPTEMBER 17

Why, my soul, are you downcast? Why so disturbed
within me? Put your hope in God, for I will yet
praise him, my Savior and my God.
Psalm 42:11

How Does This Scripture Speak To You?

_____
_____
_____
_____
_____

In What Ways Can You Apply This To Your Life?

_____
_____
_____
_____
_____

Who Could You Pray For Right Now Based On This Scripture?

_____
_____
_____
_____

SEPTEMBER 18

It is written: 'As surely as I live,' says the Lord,
'every knee will bow before me;
every tongue will acknowledge God.'
Romans 14:11

How Does This Scripture Speak To You?

_____

_____

_____

_____

_____

In What Ways Can You Apply This To Your Life?

_____

_____

_____

_____

Who Could You Pray For Right Now Based On This Scripture?

_____

_____

_____

_____

SEPTEMBER 19

Give praise to the Lord, proclaim his name;
make known among the nations what he has done.
Psalm 105:1

How Does This Scripture Speak To You?

_____
_____
_____
_____
_____

In What Ways Can You Apply This To Your Life?

_____
_____
_____
_____
_____

Who Could You Pray For Right Now Based On This Scripture?

_____
_____
_____
_____

SEPTEMBER 20

I spread out my hands to you;
I thirst for you like a parched land.
Psalm 143:6

How Does This Scripture Speak To You?

_____

_____

_____

_____

_____

In What Ways Can You Apply This To Your Life?

_____

_____

_____

_____

_____

Who Could You Pray For Right Now Based On This Scripture?

_____

_____

_____

_____

SEPTEMBER 21

Come, let us bow down in worship,
let us kneel before the Lord our Maker.
Psalm 95:6

How Does This Scripture Speak To You?

_____
_____
_____
_____
_____

In What Ways Can You Apply This To Your Life?

_____
_____
_____
_____
_____

Who Could You Pray For Right Now Based On This Scripture?

_____
_____
_____
_____

SEPTEMBER 22

There is no one holy like the Lord;
there is no one besides you;
there is no Rock like our God.
1 Samuel 2:2

How Does This Scripture Speak To You?

_____

_____

_____

_____

_____

In What Ways Can You Apply This To Your Life?

_____

_____

_____

_____

_____

Who Could You Pray For Right Now Based On This Scripture?

_____

_____

_____

_____

SEPTEMBER 23

I cried out to him with my mouth;
his praise was on my tongue.
Psalm 66:17

How Does This Scripture Speak To You?

_____
_____
_____
_____
_____

In What Ways Can You Apply This To Your Life?

_____
_____
_____
_____
_____

Who Could You Pray For Right Now Based On This Scripture?

_____
_____
_____
_____

SEPTEMBER 24

I say to the Lord, "You are my Lord;
apart from you I have no good thing."
Psalm 16:2

How Does This Scripture Speak To You?

_____
_____
_____
_____
_____

In What Ways Can You Apply This To Your Life?

_____
_____
_____
_____
_____

Who Could You Pray For Right Now Based On This Scripture?

_____
_____
_____
_____

SEPTEMBER 25

Now I, Nebuchadnezzar, praise and exalt and glorify the King of heaven, because everything he does is right and all his ways are just. And those who walk in pride he is able to humble.

Daniel 4:37

How Does This Scripture Speak To You?

_____

_____

_____

_____

_____

In What Ways Can You Apply This To Your Life?

_____

_____

_____

_____

_____

Who Could You Pray For Right Now Based On This Scripture?

_____

_____

_____

_____

SEPTEMBER 26

Out of the same mouth come praise and cursing. My
brothers and sisters, this should not be.
James 3:10

How Does This Scripture Speak To You?

_____
_____
_____
_____
_____

In What Ways Can You Apply This To Your Life?

_____
_____
_____
_____

Who Could You Pray For Right Now Based On This Scripture?

_____
_____
_____
_____

SEPTEMBER 27

Because your love is better than life,
my lips will glorify you.
I will praise you as long as I live,
and in your name I will lift up my hands.
Psalm 63:3-4

How Does This Scripture Speak To You?

_____
_____
_____
_____
_____

In What Ways Can You Apply This To Your Life?

_____
_____
_____
_____
_____

Who Could You Pray For Right Now Based On This Scripture?

_____
_____
_____
_____

SEPTEMBER 28

Now to him who is able to do immeasurably more than all we ask or imagine, according to his power that is at work within us, to him be glory in the church and in Christ Jesus throughout all generations, for ever and ever! Amen.
Ephesians 3:20-21

How Does This Scripture Speak To You?

_____
_____
_____
_____
_____

In What Ways Can You Apply This To Your Life?

_____
_____
_____
_____
_____

Who Could You Pray For Right Now Based On This Scripture?

_____
_____
_____
_____

SEPTEMBER 29

Then I heard every creature in heaven and on earth and under the earth and on the sea, and all that is in them, saying: "To him who sits on the throne and to the Lamb be praise and honor and glory and power, for ever and ever!" Revelation 5:13

How Does This Scripture Speak To You?

_____
_____
_____
_____
_____

In What Ways Can You Apply This To Your Life?

_____
_____
_____
_____
_____

Who Could You Pray For Right Now Based On This Scripture?

_____
_____
_____
_____

SEPTEMBER 30

The Lord is my strength and my shield;
my heart trusts in him, and he helps me.
My heart leaps for joy,
and with my song I praise him.
Psalm 28:7

How Does This Scripture Speak To You?

_____
_____
_____
_____
_____

In What Ways Can You Apply This To Your Life?

_____
_____
_____
_____

Who Could You Pray For Right Now Based On This Scripture?

_____
_____
_____

October

Righteousness Scriptures

OCTOBER 1

Whoever pursues righteousness and love
finds life, prosperity and honor.
Proverbs 21:21

How Does This Scripture Speak To You?

_____

_____

_____

_____

_____

In What Ways Can You Apply This To Your Life?

_____

_____

_____

_____

_____

Who Could You Pray For Right Now Based On This Scripture?

_____

_____

_____

_____

OCTOBER 2

God "will repay each person according to what they have done."
Romans 2:6

How Does This Scripture Speak To You?

_____

_____

_____

_____

_____

In What Ways Can You Apply This To Your Life?

_____

_____

_____

_____

_____

Who Could You Pray For Right Now Based On This Scripture?

_____

_____

_____

_____

OCTOBER 3

But you, man of God, flee from all this, and pursue righteousness, godliness, faith, love, endurance and gentleness.
1 Timothy 6:11

How Does This Scripture Speak To You?

_____
_____
_____
_____
_____

In What Ways Can You Apply This To Your Life?

_____
_____
_____
_____
_____

Who Could You Pray For Right Now Based On This Scripture?

_____
_____
_____
_____

OCTOBER 4

For the Lord loves the just
and will not forsake his faithful ones.
Wrongdoers will be completely destroyed;
the offspring of the wicked will perish.
Psalm 37:28

How Does This Scripture Speak To You?

_____
_____
_____
_____
_____

In What Ways Can You Apply This To Your Life?

_____
_____
_____
_____
_____

Who Could You Pray For Right Now Based On This Scripture?

_____
_____
_____
_____

OCTOBER 5

Do not be deceived: God cannot be mocked. A
man reaps what he sows.
<u>Galatians 6:7</u>

How Does This Scripture Speak To You?

_____

_____

_____

_____

_____

In What Ways Can You Apply This To Your Life?

_____

_____

_____

_____

_____

**Who Could You Pray For Right Now Based On
This Scripture?**

_____

_____

_____

_____

OCTOBER 6

A person may think their own ways are right,
but the Lord weighs the heart.
Proverbs 21:2

How Does This Scripture Speak To You?

_____

_____

_____

_____

_____

In What Ways Can You Apply This To Your Life?

_____

_____

_____

_____

_____

**Who Could You Pray For Right Now Based On
This Scripture?**

_____

_____

_____

_____

OCTOBER 7

Surely the righteous will never be shaken;
they will be remembered forever.
Psalm 112:6

How Does This Scripture Speak To You?

_____
_____
_____
_____
_____

In What Ways Can You Apply This To Your Life?

_____
_____
_____
_____
_____

Who Could You Pray For Right Now Based On This Scripture?

_____
_____
_____
_____

OCTOBER 8

But seek first his kingdom and his righteousness,
and all these things will be given to you as well.
Matthew 6:33

How Does This Scripture Speak To You?

_____
_____
_____
_____
_____

In What Ways Can You Apply This To Your Life?

_____
_____
_____
_____
_____

Who Could You Pray For Right Now Based On This Scripture?

_____
_____
_____
_____

OCTOBER 9

To do what is right and just
is more acceptable to the Lord than sacrifice.
Proverbs 21:3

How Does This Scripture Speak To You?

_____

_____

_____

_____

_____

In What Ways Can You Apply This To Your Life?

_____

_____

_____

_____

_____

Who Could You Pray For Right Now Based On This Scripture?

_____

_____

_____

_____

OCTOBER 10

But even if you should suffer for what is right, you are blessed. "Do not fear their threats; do not be frightened."
1 Peter 3:14

How Does This Scripture Speak To You?

_____
_____
_____
_____
_____

In What Ways Can You Apply This To Your Life?

_____
_____
_____
_____
_____

Who Could You Pray For Right Now Based On This Scripture?

_____
_____
_____
_____

OCTOBER 11

Let us not become weary in doing good, for at the proper time we will reap a harvest if we do not give up.
Galatians 6:9

How Does This Scripture Speak To You?

_____

_____

_____

_____

_____

In What Ways Can You Apply This To Your Life?

_____

_____

_____

_____

_____

Who Could You Pray For Right Now Based On This Scripture?

_____

_____

_____

_____

OCTOBER 12

The eyes of the Lord are on the righteous,
and his ears are attentive to their cry.
Psalm 34:15

How Does This Scripture Speak To You?

_____
_____
_____
_____
_____

In What Ways Can You Apply This To Your Life?

_____
_____
_____
_____
_____

Who Could You Pray For Right Now Based On This Scripture?

_____
_____
_____
_____

OCTOBER 13

God made him who had no sin to be sin for us, so that in him we might become the righteousness of God.
2 Corinthians 5:21

How Does This Scripture Speak To You?

_____

_____

_____

_____

_____

In What Ways Can You Apply This To Your Life?

_____

_____

_____

_____

_____

Who Could You Pray For Right Now Based On This Scripture?

_____

_____

_____

_____

OCTOBER 14

Make sure that nobody pays back wrong for wrong,
but always strive to do what is good for each other
and for everyone else.
1 Thessalonians 5:15

How Does This Scripture Speak To You?

_____
_____
_____
_____
_____

In What Ways Can You Apply This To Your Life?

_____
_____
_____
_____
_____

Who Could You Pray For Right Now Based On This Scripture?

_____
_____
_____
_____

OCTOBER 15

Finally, brothers and sisters, whatever is true, whatever is noble, whatever is right, whatever is pure, whatever is lovely, whatever is admirable—if anything is excellent or praiseworthy—think about such things.
Philippians 4:8

How Does This Scripture Speak To You?

_____
_____
_____
_____
_____

In What Ways Can You Apply This To Your Life?

_____
_____
_____
_____
_____

Who Could You Pray For Right Now Based On This Scripture?

_____
_____
_____
_____

OCTOBER 16

For the grace of God has appeared that offers salvation to all people. It teaches us to say "No" to ungodliness and worldly passions, and to live self-controlled, upright and godly lives in this present age.
Titus 2:11-12

How Does This Scripture Speak To You?

_____

_____

_____

_____

_____

In What Ways Can You Apply This To Your Life?

_____

_____

_____

_____

_____

Who Could You Pray For Right Now Based On This Scripture?

_____

_____

_____

_____

OCTOBER 17

Ill-gotten treasures have no lasting value,
but righteousness delivers from death.
Proverbs 10:2

How Does This Scripture Speak To You?

_____
_____
_____
_____
_____

In What Ways Can You Apply This To Your Life?

_____
_____
_____
_____
_____

**Who Could You Pray For Right Now Based On
This Scripture?**

_____
_____
_____
_____

OCTOBER 18

Blessed is the one who does not walk in step with the
wicked or stand in the way that sinners take
or sit in the company of mockers.
Psalm 1:1

How Does This Scripture Speak To You?

_____
_____
_____
_____
_____

In What Ways Can You Apply This To Your Life?

_____
_____
_____
_____

Who Could You Pray For Right Now Based On This Scripture?

_____
_____
_____
_____

OCTOBER 19

Peacemakers who sow in peace reap a harvest of
righteousness.
James 3:18

How Does This Scripture Speak To You?

_____

_____

_____

_____

_____

In What Ways Can You Apply This To Your Life?

_____

_____

_____

_____

_____

Who Could You Pray For Right Now Based On This Scripture?

_____

_____

_____

_____

OCTOBER 20

A wicked person earns deceptive wages,
but the one who sows righteousness reaps a
sure reward.
Proverbs 11:18

How Does This Scripture Speak To You?

_____
_____
_____
_____
_____

In What Ways Can You Apply This To Your Life?

_____
_____
_____
_____
_____

Who Could You Pray For Right Now Based On This Scripture?

_____
_____
_____
_____

OCTOBER 21

And if you do good to those who are good to you,
what credit is that to you? Even sinners do that.
Luke 6:33

How Does This Scripture Speak To You?

_____
_____
_____
_____
_____

In What Ways Can You Apply This To Your Life?

_____
_____
_____
_____
_____

Who Could You Pray For Right Now Based On This Scripture?

_____
_____
_____
_____

OCTOBER 22

Therefore confess your sins to each other and pray for each other so that you may be healed. The prayer of a righteous person is powerful and effective.
James 5:16

How Does This Scripture Speak To You?

_____

_____

_____

_____

_____

In What Ways Can You Apply This To Your Life?

_____

_____

_____

_____

_____

Who Could You Pray For Right Now Based On This Scripture?

_____

_____

_____

_____

OCTOBER 23

I seek you with all my heart;
do not let me stray from your commands.
Psalm 119:10

How Does This Scripture Speak To You?

_____
_____
_____
_____
_____

In What Ways Can You Apply This To Your Life?

_____
_____
_____
_____
_____

Who Could You Pray For Right Now Based On This Scripture?

_____
_____
_____
_____

OCTOBER 24

It is a trap to dedicate something rashly
and only later to consider one's vows.
Proverbs 20:25

How Does This Scripture Speak To You?

_____

_____

_____

_____

_____

In What Ways Can You Apply This To Your Life?

_____

_____

_____

_____

**Who Could You Pray For Right Now Based On
This Scripture?**

_____

_____

_____

_____

OCTOBER 25

Come near to God and he will come near to you.
Wash your hands, you sinners, and purify your hearts,
you double-minded.
James 4:8

How Does This Scripture Speak To You?

_____
_____
_____
_____
_____

In What Ways Can You Apply This To Your Life?

_____
_____
_____
_____
_____

Who Could You Pray For Right Now Based On This Scripture?

_____
_____
_____
_____

OCTOBER 26

Blessed are those who hunger and thirst for righteousness, for they will be filled.
Matthew 5:6

How Does This Scripture Speak To You?

_____
_____
_____
_____
_____

In What Ways Can You Apply This To Your Life?

_____
_____
_____
_____
_____

Who Could You Pray For Right Now Based On This Scripture?

_____
_____
_____
_____

OCTOBER 27

Commit your way to the Lord;
trust in him and he will do this: He will make your
righteous reward shine like the dawn,
your vindication like the noonday sun.
Psalm 37:5-6

How Does This Scripture Speak To You?

_____
_____
_____
_____
_____

In What Ways Can You Apply This To Your Life?

_____
_____
_____
_____
_____

**Who Could You Pray For Right Now Based On
This Scripture?**

_____
_____
_____
_____

OCTOBER 28

The righteous person may have many troubles,
but the Lord delivers him from them all.
Psalm 34:19

How Does This Scripture Speak To You?

_____
_____
_____
_____
_____

In What Ways Can You Apply This To Your Life?

_____
_____
_____
_____
_____

**Who Could You Pray For Right Now Based On
This Scripture?**

_____
_____
_____
_____

OCTOBER 29

Speak up and judge fairly;
defend the rights of the poor and needy.
Proverbs 31:9

How Does This Scripture Speak To You?

_____
_____
_____
_____
_____

In What Ways Can You Apply This To Your Life?

_____
_____
_____
_____
_____

Who Could You Pray For Right Now Based On This Scripture?

_____
_____
_____
_____

OCTOBER 30

"No weapon forged against you will prevail, and you will refute every tongue that accuses you. This is the heritage of the servants of the Lord, and this is their vindication from me," declares the Lord.
Isaiah 54:17

How Does This Scripture Speak To You?

_____

_____

_____

_____

_____

In What Ways Can You Apply This To Your Life?

_____

_____

_____

_____

_____

Who Could You Pray For Right Now Based On This Scripture?

_____

_____

_____

_____

OCTOBER 31

You, therefore, have no excuse, you who pass judgment on someone else, for at whatever point you judge another, you are condemning yourself, because you who pass judgment do the same things.
<u>Romans 2:1</u>

How Does This Scripture Speak To You?

_____

_____

_____

_____

_____

In What Ways Can You Apply This To Your Life?

_____

_____

_____

_____

_____

Who Could You Pray For Right Now Based On This Scripture?

_____

_____

_____

_____

November

Love Scriptures

NOVEMBER 1

Love is patient, love is kind. It does not envy, it does not boast, it is not proud. It does not dishonor others, it is not self-seeking, it is not easily angered, it keeps no record of wrongs.
1 Corinthians 13:4-5

How Does This Scripture Speak To You?

_____
_____
_____
_____
_____

In What Ways Can You Apply This To Your Life?

_____
_____
_____
_____
_____

Who Could You Pray For Right Now Based On This Scripture?

_____
_____
_____
_____

NOVEMBER 2

Do everything in love.
1 Corinthians 16:14

How Does This Scripture Speak To You?

_____

_____

_____

_____

_____

In What Ways Can You Apply This To Your Life?

_____

_____

_____

_____

_____

Who Could You Pray For Right Now Based On This Scripture?

_____

_____

_____

_____

NOVEMBER 3

Let the morning bring me word of your unfailing love,
for I have put my trust in you. Show me the way I
should go, for to you I entrust my life.
Psalm 143:8

How Does This Scripture Speak To You?

_____

_____

_____

_____

_____

In What Ways Can You Apply This To Your Life?

_____

_____

_____

_____

_____

Who Could You Pray For Right Now Based On This Scripture?

_____

_____

_____

_____

NOVEMBER 4

And over all these virtues put on love, which binds
them all together in perfect unity.
Colossians 3:14

How Does This Scripture Speak To You?

_____

_____

_____

_____

_____

In What Ways Can You Apply This To Your Life?

_____

_____

_____

_____

_____

Who Could You Pray For Right Now Based On This Scripture?

_____

_____

_____

_____

NOVEMBER 5

Let love and faithfulness never leave you; bind them around your neck, write them on the tablet of your heart. Then you will win favor and a good name in the sight of God and man.
Proverbs 3:3-4

How Does This Scripture Speak To You?

_____

_____

_____

_____

_____

In What Ways Can You Apply This To Your Life?

_____

_____

_____

_____

_____

Who Could You Pray For Right Now Based On This Scripture?

_____

_____

_____

_____

NOVEMBER 6

And so we know and rely on the love God has for us.
God is love. Whoever lives in love lives in God, and
God in them.
1 John 4:16

How Does This Scripture Speak To You?

_____

_____

_____

_____

_____

In What Ways Can You Apply This To Your Life?

_____

_____

_____

_____

_____

**Who Could You Pray For Right Now Based On
This Scripture?**

_____

_____

_____

_____

NOVEMBER 7

Be completely humble and gentle; be patient,
bearing with one another in love.
Ephesians 4:2

How Does This Scripture Speak To You?

_____

_____

_____

_____

_____

In What Ways Can You Apply This To Your Life?

_____

_____

_____

_____

_____

Who Could You Pray For Right Now Based On This Scripture?

_____

_____

_____

_____

NOVEMBER 8

We love because He first loved us.
1 John 4:19

How Does This Scripture Speak To You?

_____
_____
_____
_____
_____

In What Ways Can You Apply This To Your Life?

_____
_____
_____
_____
_____

Who Could You Pray For Right Now Based On This Scripture?

_____
_____
_____
_____

NOVEMBER 9

And now these three remain: faith, hope and love.
But the greatest of these is love.
1 Corinthians 13:13

How Does This Scripture Speak To You?

_____
_____
_____
_____
_____

In What Ways Can You Apply This To Your Life?

_____
_____
_____
_____
_____

Who Could You Pray For Right Now Based On This Scripture?

_____
_____
_____
_____

NOVEMBER 10

Above all, love each other deeply, because love
covers over a multitude of sins.
<u>1 Peter 4:8</u>

How Does This Scripture Speak To You?

_____
_____
_____
_____
_____

In What Ways Can You Apply This To Your Life?

_____
_____
_____
_____
_____

Who Could You Pray For Right Now Based On This Scripture?

_____
_____
_____
_____

NOVEMBER 11

I pray that out of his glorious riches he may strengthen you with power through his Spirit in your inner being, so that Christ may dwell in your hearts through faith. And I pray that you, being rooted and established in love.

Ephesians 3:16-17

How Does This Scripture Speak To You?

_____

_____

_____

_____

_____

In What Ways Can You Apply This To Your Life?

_____

_____

_____

_____

_____

Who Could You Pray For Right Now Based On This Scripture?

_____

_____

_____

_____

NOVEMBER 12

Love must be sincere. Hate what is evil; cling to
what is good.
Romans 12:9

How Does This Scripture Speak To You?

_____
_____
_____
_____
_____

In What Ways Can You Apply This To Your Life?

_____
_____
_____
_____
_____

Who Could You Pray For Right Now Based On
This Scripture?

_____
_____
_____
_____

NOVEMBER 13

If I have the gift of prophecy and can fathom all
mysteries and all knowledge, and if I have a faith
that can move mountains, but do not have love, I am
nothing. 1 Corinthians 13:2

How Does This Scripture Speak To You?

_____

_____

_____

_____

_____

In What Ways Can You Apply This To Your Life?

_____

_____

_____

_____

Who Could You Pray For Right Now Based On This Scripture?

_____

_____

_____

_____

NOVEMBER 14

My command is this: Love each other as I have loved you.
John 15:12

How Does This Scripture Speak To You?

_____

_____

_____

_____

_____

In What Ways Can You Apply This To Your Life?

_____

_____

_____

_____

_____

Who Could You Pray For Right Now Based On This Scripture?

_____

_____

_____

_____

NOVEMBER 15

Can a mother forget the baby at her breast and have no compassion on the child she has borne? Though she may forget, I will not forget you! See, I have engraved you on the palms of my hands; your walls are ever before me. Isaiah 49:15-16

How Does This Scripture Speak To You?

_____
_____
_____
_____
_____

In What Ways Can You Apply This To Your Life?

_____
_____
_____
_____
_____

Who Could You Pray For Right Now Based On This Scripture?

_____
_____
_____
_____

NOVEMBER 16

Be devoted to one another in love. Honor one
another above yourselves.
Romans 12:10

How Does This Scripture Speak To You?

_____
_____
_____
_____
_____

In What Ways Can You Apply This To Your Life?

_____
_____
_____
_____
_____

Who Could You Pray For Right Now Based On This Scripture?

_____
_____
_____
_____

NOVEMBER 17

Husbands, love your wives, just as Christ loved the church and gave himself up for her to make her holy, cleansing her by the washing with water through the word.
Ephesians 5:25-26

How Does This Scripture Speak To You?

_____
_____
_____
_____
_____

In What Ways Can You Apply This To Your Life?

_____
_____
_____
_____
_____

Who Could You Pray For Right Now Based On This Scripture?

_____
_____
_____
_____

NOVEMBER 18

May the Lord direct your hearts into God's
love and Christ's perseverance.
2 Thessalonians 3:5

How Does This Scripture Speak To You?

_____
_____
_____
_____
_____

In What Ways Can You Apply This To Your Life?

_____
_____
_____
_____
_____

Who Could You Pray For Right Now Based On This Scripture?

_____
_____
_____
_____

NOVEMBER 19

No one has ever seen God; but if we love one another,
God lives in us and his love is made complete in us.
1 John 4:12

How Does This Scripture Speak To You?

_____

_____

_____

_____

_____

In What Ways Can You Apply This To Your Life?

_____

_____

_____

_____

_____

Who Could You Pray For Right Now Based On This Scripture?

_____

_____

_____

_____

NOVEMBER 20

Whoever claims to love God yet hates a brother or sister is a liar. For whoever does not love their brother and sister, whom they have seen, cannot love God, whom they have not seen.
1 John 4:20

How Does This Scripture Speak To You?

_____
_____
_____
_____
_____

In What Ways Can You Apply This To Your Life?

_____
_____
_____
_____
_____

Who Could You Pray For Right Now Based On This Scripture?

_____
_____
_____
_____

NOVEMBER 21

Greater love has no one than this: to lay down
one's life for one's friends.
John 15:13

How Does This Scripture Speak To You?

_____

_____

_____

_____

_____

In What Ways Can You Apply This To Your Life?

_____

_____

_____

_____

_____

Who Could You Pray For Right Now Based On This Scripture?

_____

_____

_____

_____

NOVEMBER 22

Since you are precious and honored in my sight,
and because I love you,
I will give people in exchange for you,
nations in exchange for your life.
Isaiah 43:4

How Does This Scripture Speak To You?

_____

_____

_____

_____

_____

In What Ways Can You Apply This To Your Life?

_____

_____

_____

_____

_____

Who Could You Pray For Right Now Based On This Scripture?

_____

_____

_____

_____

NOVEMBER 23

However, as it is written: What no eye has seen,
what no ear has heard, and what no human mind
has conceived — the things God has prepared
for those who love him.
1 Corinthians 2:9

How Does This Scripture Speak To You?

_____

_____

_____

_____

_____

In What Ways Can You Apply This To Your Life?

_____

_____

_____

_____

_____

**Who Could You Pray For Right Now Based On
This Scripture?**

_____

_____

_____

_____

NOVEMBER 24

Let no debt remain outstanding, except the continuing debt to love one another, for whoever loves others has fulfilled the law.
Romans 13:8

How Does This Scripture Speak To You?

_____

_____

_____

_____

_____

In What Ways Can You Apply This To Your Life?

_____

_____

_____

_____

_____

Who Could You Pray For Right Now Based On This Scripture?

_____

_____

_____

_____

NOVEMBER 25

See what great love the Father has lavished on us,
that we should be called children of God! And that
is what we are! The reason the world does not
know us is that it did not know him.
1 John 3:1

How Does This Scripture Speak To You?

_____

_____

_____

_____

_____

In What Ways Can You Apply This To Your Life?

_____

_____

_____

_____

_____

Who Could You Pray For Right Now Based On This Scripture?

_____

_____

_____

_____

NOVEMBER 26

There is no fear in love. But perfect love drives out fear, because fear has to do with punishment. The one who fears is not made perfect in love.
1 John 4:18

How Does This Scripture Speak To You?

_____
_____
_____
_____
_____

In What Ways Can You Apply This To Your Life?

_____
_____
_____
_____
_____

Who Could You Pray For Right Now Based On This Scripture?

_____
_____
_____
_____

NOVEMBER 27

May the Lord make your love increase and overflow
for each other and for everyone else, just as ours
does for you.
1 Thessalonians 3:12

How Does This Scripture Speak To You?

_____
_____
_____
_____
_____

In What Ways Can You Apply This To Your Life?

_____
_____
_____
_____

Who Could You Pray For Right Now Based On This Scripture?

_____
_____
_____
_____

NOVEMBER 28

Place me like a seal over your heart, like a seal on your arm; for love is as strong as death, its jealousy unyielding as the grave. It burns like blazing fire, like a mighty flame.
<u>Song of songs 8:6</u>

How Does This Scripture Speak To You?

_____
_____
_____
_____
_____

In What Ways Can You Apply This To Your Life?

_____
_____
_____
_____
_____

Who Could You Pray For Right Now Based On This Scripture?

_____
_____
_____
_____

NOVEMBER 29

Whoever pursues righteousness and love
finds life, prosperity and honor.
Proverbs 21:21

How Does This Scripture Speak To You?

_____
_____
_____
_____
_____

In What Ways Can You Apply This To Your Life?

_____
_____
_____
_____
_____

Who Could You Pray For Right Now Based On This Scripture?

_____
_____
_____
_____

NOVEMBER 30

Hatred stirs up conflict,
but love covers over all wrongs.
Proverbs 10:12

How Does This Scripture Speak To You?

_____
_____
_____
_____
_____

In What Ways Can You Apply This To Your Life?

_____
_____
_____
_____
_____

Who Could You Pray For Right Now Based On This Scripture?

_____
_____
_____
_____

December

Salvation Scriptures

DECEMBER 1

Salvation is found in no one else, for there is no other name under heaven given to mankind by which we must be saved.
Acts 4:12

How Does This Scripture Speak To You?

_____

_____

_____

_____

_____

In What Ways Can You Apply This To Your Life?

_____

_____

_____

_____

_____

Who Could You Pray For Right Now Based On This Scripture?

_____

_____

_____

_____

DECEMBER 2

They replied, "Believe in the Lord Jesus, and you
will be saved—you and your household."
Acts 16:31

How Does This Scripture Speak To You?

_____

_____

_____

_____

_____

In What Ways Can You Apply This To Your Life?

_____

_____

_____

_____

_____

Who Could You Pray For Right Now Based On This Scripture?

_____

_____

_____

_____

DECEMBER 3

He has saved us and called us to a holy life—not because of anything we have done but because of his own purpose and grace. This grace was given us in Christ Jesus before the beginning of time.
2 Timothy 1:9

How Does This Scripture Speak To You?

_____
_____
_____
_____
_____

In What Ways Can You Apply This To Your Life?

_____
_____
_____
_____
_____

Who Could You Pray For Right Now Based On This Scripture?

_____
_____
_____
_____

DECEMBER 4

Truly my soul finds rest in God;
my salvation comes from him.
Psalm 62:1

How Does This Scripture Speak To You?

_____

_____

_____

_____

_____

In What Ways Can You Apply This To Your Life?

_____

_____

_____

_____

_____

Who Could You Pray For Right Now Based On This Scripture?

_____

_____

_____

_____

DECEMBER 5

And everyone who calls on the name of the
Lord will be saved.
Acts 2:21

How Does This Scripture Speak To You?

_____
_____
_____
_____
_____

In What Ways Can You Apply This To Your Life?

_____
_____
_____
_____

Who Could You Pray For Right Now Based On This Scripture?

_____
_____
_____
_____

DECEMBER 6

Or do you not know that wrongdoers will not inherit the kingdom of God? Do not be deceived: Neither the sexually immoral nor idolaters nor adulterers nor men who have sex with men nor thieves nor the greedy nor drunkards nor slanderers nor swindlers will inherit the kingdom of God.
1 Corinthians 6:9-10

How Does This Scripture Speak To You?

_____
_____
_____
_____
_____

In What Ways Can You Apply This To Your Life?

_____
_____
_____
_____
_____

Who Could You Pray For Right Now Based On This Scripture?

_____
_____
_____
_____

DECEMBER 7

For it is with your heart that you believe and are
justified, and it is with your mouth that you profess
your faith and are saved.
Romans 10:10

How Does This Scripture Speak To You?

_____

_____

_____

_____

_____

In What Ways Can You Apply This To Your Life?

_____

_____

_____

_____

Who Could You Pray For Right Now Based On This Scripture?

_____

_____

_____

_____

DECEMBER 8

For the grace of God has appeared that offers salvation
to all people. It teaches us to say "No" to ungodliness
and worldly passions, and to live self-controlled,
upright and godly lives in this present age.
Titus 2:11-12

How Does This Scripture Speak To You?

_____

_____

_____

_____

_____

In What Ways Can You Apply This To Your Life?

_____

_____

_____

_____

_____

**Who Could You Pray For Right Now Based On
This Scripture?**

_____

_____

_____

_____

DECEMBER 9

The Lord is not slow in keeping his promise, as some understand slowness. Instead he is patient with you, not wanting anyone to perish, but everyone to come to repentance.
2 Peter 3:9

How Does This Scripture Speak To You?

_____
_____
_____
_____
_____

In What Ways Can You Apply This To Your Life?

_____
_____
_____
_____
_____

Who Could You Pray For Right Now Based On This Scripture?

_____
_____
_____
_____

DECEMBER 10

For the Son of Man came to seek and to save
the lost.
Luke 19:10

How Does This Scripture Speak To You?

_____

_____

_____

_____

_____

In What Ways Can You Apply This To Your Life?

_____

_____

_____

_____

_____

Who Could You Pray For Right Now Based On This Scripture?

_____

_____

_____

_____

DECEMBER 11

Jesus replied, "What is impossible with man
is possible with God."
Luke 18:27

How Does This Scripture Speak To You?

_____

_____

_____

_____

_____

In What Ways Can You Apply This To Your Life?

_____

_____

_____

_____

_____

**Who Could You Pray For Right Now Based On
This Scripture?**

_____

_____

_____

_____

DECEMBER 12

Whoever believes and is baptized will be saved, but whoever does not believe will be condemned.
Mark 16:16

How Does This Scripture Speak To You?

_____
_____
_____
_____
_____

In What Ways Can You Apply This To Your Life?

_____
_____
_____
_____
_____

Who Could You Pray For Right Now Based On This Scripture?

_____
_____
_____
_____

DECEMBER 13

Though you have not seen him, you love him; and even though you do not see him now, you believe in him and are filled with an inexpressible and glorious joy, for you are receiving the end result of your faith, the salvation of your souls.
1 Peter 1:8-9

How Does This Scripture Speak To You?

_____
_____
_____
_____
_____

In What Ways Can You Apply This To Your Life?

_____
_____
_____
_____

Who Could You Pray For Right Now Based On This Scripture?

_____
_____
_____

DECEMBER 14

Enter through the narrow gate. For wide is the gate
and broad is the road that leads to destruction, and
many enter through it. But small is the gate and narrow
the road that leads to life, and only a few find it.
Matthew 7:13-14

How Does This Scripture Speak To You?

_____

_____

_____

_____

_____

In What Ways Can You Apply This To Your Life?

_____

_____

_____

_____

_____

Who Could You Pray For Right Now Based On This Scripture?

_____

_____

_____

_____

DECEMBER 15

So Christ was sacrificed once to take away the sins of
many; and he will appear a second time, not to
bear sin, but to bring salvation to those who
are waiting for him.
Hebrews 9:28

How Does This Scripture Speak To You?

_____
_____
_____
_____
_____

In What Ways Can You Apply This To Your Life?

_____
_____
_____
_____
_____

Who Could You Pray For Right Now Based On This Scripture?

_____
_____
_____
_____

DECEMBER 16

For this is what the Lord has commanded us:
"I have made you a light for the Gentiles,
that you may bring salvation to the ends of the earth."
Acts 13:47

How Does This Scripture Speak To You?

_____

_____

_____

_____

_____

In What Ways Can You Apply This To Your Life?

_____

_____

_____

_____

_____

Who Could You Pray For Right Now Based On This Scripture?

_____

_____

_____

_____

DECEMBER 17

For I am not ashamed of the gospel, because it is the power of God that brings salvation to everyone who believes: first to the Jew, then to the Gentile.
Romans 1:16

How Does This Scripture Speak To You?

_____
_____
_____
_____
_____

In What Ways Can You Apply This To Your Life?

_____
_____
_____
_____
_____

Who Could You Pray For Right Now Based On This Scripture?

_____
_____
_____
_____

DECEMBER 18

Very rarely will anyone die for a righteous person, though for a good person someone might possibly dare to die. But God demonstrates his own love for us in this: While we were still sinners, Christ died for us.
Romans 5:7-8

How Does This Scripture Speak To You?

_____
_____
_____
_____
_____

In What Ways Can You Apply This To Your Life?

_____
_____
_____
_____
_____

Who Could You Pray For Right Now Based On This Scripture?

_____
_____
_____
_____

DECEMBER 19

For as in Adam all die, so in Christ all will
be made alive.
1 Corinthians 15:22

How Does This Scripture Speak To You?

_____

_____

_____

_____

_____

In What Ways Can You Apply This To Your Life?

_____

_____

_____

_____

**Who Could You Pray For Right Now Based On
This Scripture?**

_____

_____

_____

_____

DECEMBER 20

Jesus looked at them and said, "With man this is impossible, but not with God; all things are possible with God."
Mark 10:27

How Does This Scripture Speak To You?

_____
_____
_____
_____
_____

In What Ways Can You Apply This To Your Life?

_____
_____
_____
_____
_____

Who Could You Pray For Right Now Based On This Scripture?

_____
_____
_____
_____

DECEMBER 21

You make your saving help my shield, and your right
hand sustains me; your help has made me great.
You provide a broad path for my feet,
so that my ankles do not give way.
Psalm 18:35-36

How Does This Scripture Speak To You?

_____
_____
_____
_____
_____

In What Ways Can You Apply This To Your Life?

_____
_____
_____
_____
_____

Who Could You Pray For Right Now Based On This Scripture?

_____
_____
_____
_____

DECEMBER 22

The righteous cry out, and the Lord hears them;
he delivers them from all their troubles.
The Lord is close to the brokenhearted
and saves those who are crushed in spirit.
Psalm 34:17-18

How Does This Scripture Speak To You?

_____
_____
_____
_____
_____

In What Ways Can You Apply This To Your Life?

_____
_____
_____
_____

Who Could You Pray For Right Now Based On This Scripture?

_____
_____
_____
_____

DECEMBER 23

For if, while we were God's enemies, we were
reconciled to him through the death of his Son, how
much more, having been reconciled, shall we
be saved through his life!
Romans 5:10

How Does This Scripture Speak To You?

_____
_____
_____
_____
_____

In What Ways Can You Apply This To Your Life?

_____
_____
_____
_____

**Who Could You Pray For Right Now Based On
This Scripture?**

_____
_____
_____
_____

DECEMBER 24

"Go," said Jesus, "your faith has healed you."
Immediately he received his sight and followed
Jesus along the road.
Mark 10:52

How Does This Scripture Speak To You?

_____
_____
_____
_____
_____

In What Ways Can You Apply This To Your Life?

_____
_____
_____
_____
_____

Who Could You Pray For Right Now Based On This Scripture?

_____
_____
_____
_____

DECEMBER 25

Since you are precious and honored in my sight,
and because I love you, I will give people in exchange
for you, nations in exchange for your life.
Isaiah 43:4

How Does This Scripture Speak To You?

_____

_____

_____

_____

_____

In What Ways Can You Apply This To Your Life?

_____

_____

_____

_____

Who Could You Pray For Right Now Based On This Scripture?

_____

_____

_____

_____

DECEMBER 26

My salvation and my honor depend on God;
he is my mighty rock, my refuge.
Psalm 62:7

How Does This Scripture Speak To You?

_____
_____
_____
_____
_____

In What Ways Can You Apply This To Your Life?

_____
_____
_____
_____
_____

Who Could You Pray For Right Now Based On This Scripture?

_____
_____
_____
_____

DECEMBER 27

For God did not send his Son into the world to condemn the world, but to save the world through him.
John 3:17

How Does This Scripture Speak To You?

_____
_____
_____
_____
_____

In What Ways Can You Apply This To Your Life?

_____
_____
_____
_____
_____

Who Could You Pray For Right Now Based On This Scripture?

_____
_____
_____
_____

DECEMBER 28

As far as the east is from the west,
so far has he removed our transgressions from us.
Psalm 103:12

How Does This Scripture Speak To You?

_____
_____
_____
_____
_____

In What Ways Can You Apply This To Your Life?

_____
_____
_____
_____
_____

Who Could You Pray For Right Now Based On This Scripture?

_____
_____
_____
_____

DECEMBER 29

For, "Everyone who calls on the name of the
Lord will be saved."
<u>Romans 10:13</u>

How Does This Scripture Speak To You?

_____

_____

_____

_____

_____

In What Ways Can You Apply This To Your Life?

_____

_____

_____

_____

_____

Who Could You Pray For Right Now Based On This Scripture?

_____

_____

_____

_____

DECEMBER 30

Like newborn babies, crave pure spiritual milk, so that
by it you may grow up in your salvation.
1 Peter 2:2

How Does This Scripture Speak To You?

_____
_____
_____
_____
_____

In What Ways Can You Apply This To Your Life?

_____
_____
_____
_____
_____

Who Could You Pray For Right Now Based On This Scripture?

_____
_____
_____
_____

DECEMBER 31

I love you, Lord, my strength. The Lord is my rock,
my fortress and my deliverer; my God is my rock,
in whom I take refuge, my shield and the horn of my
salvation, my stronghold.
Psalm 18:1-2

How Does This Scripture Speak To You?

_____
_____
_____
_____
_____

In What Ways Can You Apply This To Your Life?

_____
_____
_____
_____
_____

Who Could You Pray For Right Now Based On This Scripture?

_____
_____
_____
_____

Hello Readers!

I'm an independent author and Amazon reviews make a huge difference to the overall success for this book! If you enjoyed this book, please consider taking a few moments to leave a quick review on Amazon.com.

Thank you!

Jessica Strauss

Made in the USA
Las Vegas, NV
15 December 2023

82664799R00216